MIRACLE
AT
MEDINAH
EUROPE'S AMAZING RYDER CUP COMEBACK

OLIVER HOLT

headline

First published in 2012
by HEADLINE PUBLISHING GROUP

1

Cataloguing in Publication Data is available from the British Library

Hardback ISBN 978 0 7553 6481 7
Trade paperback ISBN 978 0 7553 6482 4

Typeset in Bliss by Avon DataSet Ltd, Bidford-on-Avon, Warwickshire

Printed and bound in Great Britain by Clays Ltd, St Ives plc

Headline's policy is to use papers that are natural, renewable and recyclable
products and made from wood grown in sustainable forests. The logging
and manufacturing processes are expected to conform to the
environmental regulations of the country of origin.

HEADLINE PUBLISHING GROUP
An Hachette UK Company
338 Euston Road
London NW1 3BH

www.headline.co.uk
www.hachette.co.uk

MIRACLE
AT
MEDINAH
EUROPE'S AMAZING RYDER CUP COMEBACK

For my mum and dad.

Acknowledgements

My thanks, first of all, go to my literary agent David Luxton for asking me to become involved in this project and to Jonathan Taylor at Headline for commissioning it and doing such a great job in bringing it all together. I also owe a debt of gratitude to Justyn Barnes and John English for all their superb editing work and for rescuing me from a number of silly errors. And to Emily Kitchin for her politely insistent reminders of deadlines to be met. The professionalism and skill of everyone at Headline was one of the reasons this book was a treat to write. It was a pleasure to walk the beautiful course at Medinah with friends and colleagues like Paul Hayward, Martin Samuel, John Dillon, Matt Dickinson, Richard Williams, Steve Howard, Marc Aspland, Owen Slot, Charlie Sale, Patrick Collins, Malcolm Folley and Michael Atherton, all journalists I admire greatly and whose company on working trips I never tire of. Neil McLeman, the *Daily Mirror*'s golf correspondent, is one of the best colleagues anyone could wish for and provided me with valuable help for this book. So, too, even though they didn't know it, did fine writers on golf like Derek Lawrenson, Jamie Corrigan, David Facey, David Walsh, Peter Dixon, Kevin Garside, Ewan Murray, Lawrence Donegan (now gone surfing), Neil Squires, Bill Elliott,

Paul Mahoney, Mike Dickson and John Hopkins. It is always an education being around them and reading their work. My friend Mark Simpson gave me a refresher course in Irish politics and my boss at the *Daily Mirror*, Dean Morse, gave me the chance to go to Medinah and cover the 39th Ryder Cup for a newspaper it is a privilege to work for. I owe him and everyone at the *Mirror* a debt of gratitude for that, too. It was one of the best weekends of sport I have ever witnessed.

Oliver Holt
November, 2012

Contents

Introduction: Europe's 13th Man   1

Chapter 1:   Captain Love and the new Americans   17

Chapter 2:   Big hitting, freewheeling . . . but no rough
              stuff   29

Chapter 3:   Rabble-rousing in the Midwest in the fall   42

Chapter 4:   Just me and Tiger   52

Chapter 5:   Done mooching   65

Chapter 6:   America's new hero and his collection
              of idiosyncrasies   75

Chapter 7:   Bubba Golf   85

Chapter 8:   Europe's rookie steps up   95

Chapter 9:   The end of restraint   106

Chapter 10:   Phil's team   119

Chapter 11:   Blood in the water   129

Chapter 12:   Dubya and a heartbeat   140

Chapter 13:   Poulter, the defiant one   150

Chapter 14:   #whatwouldsevedo?   160

Chapter 15:   Central Time   170

Chapter 16:   Europe on the charge   180

Chapter 17:   Tangled up in blue   191

Chapter 18:   Langer, Kiawah, Kaymer   200

Chapter 19: The hollow men   208
Chapter 20: Poults Clause   224
Afterword: All men die, but not all men live   233

39th Ryder Cup Results   236
Credits   239

INTRODUCTION:
Europe's 13th Man

The 39th Ryder Cup, which was contested not far from the western shores of Lake Michigan as the greens of summer turned to the brilliant yellows of a Midwest autumn, began in May of the previous year in a village in northern Spain called Pedreña on the coast of the Bay of Biscay.

Many of the great names of European golf made a pilgrimage there to attend the funeral of Severiano Ballesteros, who had died following a long battle with brain cancer. The competition was still more than 16 months away but Pedreña was where the flame was lit.

The Ryder Cup was played out at the Medinah Country Club where the players crunched acorns underfoot as they strode the fairways during three days of sunshine and drama at the end of September 2012. But the seeds for what happened there were planted as the mourners walked down a hill to the church of San Pedro de Pedreña on an overcast spring morning in 2011, trying to come to terms with their loss.

Javier, Ballesteros's eldest son, a young man blessed with his father's smouldering good looks, carried the urn containing his ashes at the head of the funeral procession. Beside him walked his sister Carmen, bearing the branch of a magnolia tree that Ballesteros had planted in the garden of his house at the top of the hill as a lasting reminder of the glories he achieved at Augusta.

There had been a sustained round of applause from the crowds gathered outside the church as the funeral cortege arrived at the end of its short journey down the dusty country road from the house on the hill. Members of the local rowing club provided a guard of honour with raised oars – his father had been a rower and trainer at the club which carried his name – and they passed houses which had Spanish flags hanging from balconies bedecked with black ribbons.

Children from the Seve Ballesteros Foundation carried three irons aloft as a reminder of the times when he roamed the beaches with his first club, practising and practising on the sand because he was not yet allowed to play at the local club which was to become his second home, Real Golf de Pedreña.

Inside the church, his younger son, Miguel, spoke to his father. 'Papa,' he said, 'as you can see, Javier, Carmen and me are strong. Just like you asked us. For us, it's not a day to say goodbye. We know you are by our side and we will always be by yours. We love you, Dad.'

Afterwards, some of those present paid tribute to one of the greatest, most charismatic golfers the world had ever seen. Five former European Ryder Cup captains – Nick Faldo, Colin Montgomerie, Sam Torrance, Ian Woosnam and Bernard Gallacher – all spoke with great affection of the man the sporting world knew simply as Seve.

There were many tears, too, of course. Ballesteros was only 54 when he died. Many found it hard to accept he had been taken so young. Some of the contemporaneous reports, including a moving dispatch from the *Daily Telegraph*'s Ian Chadband, recorded that one of Ballesteros's former teammates was more affected than the rest. 'Somehow,' Chadband wrote, 'nobody seemed as bereft as José María Olazábal, the conjuror's old accomplice in Ryder Cup magic, who was too upset even to speak later.'

Olazábal, who had been named as the European captain for the 2012 Ryder Cup a few months earlier, had shared a particularly close bond with Ballesteros, who was nine years his senior, which went far beyond the fact that they were compatriots. It was first forged in 1987 when Olazábal made his Ryder Cup debut and Ballesteros gave him the confidence to excel.

'I was a rookie in '87 at Muirfield Village and Seve took me under his wing,' Olazábal said. 'He made it clear to Tony Jacklin [the European Ryder Cup captain] that he wanted to play with me. I will never forget that little walk from the putting green to the first tee. I was shaking like a leaf.

'They were huge crowds. Very loud. So I kept my head down, and he approached me as we were walking on to the first tee. He looked at me and said, "José María, you play your game, I'll take care of the rest." And he did. He was a great figure, I think not just for myself but for the whole European squad, not just that year but every year that he played in that team. He was a special man.'

Ballesteros and Olazábal were inseparable after that at Ryder Cups. They played 15 times together in foursomes and fourballs. They won a remarkable 11 times and lost only twice, halving the other two matches, making them the most successful combination in the history of the competition. Not surprisingly Olazábal regarded Ballesteros as a great inspiration. The Americans referred to their partnership as the Spanish Armada.

There is a famous picture of the two men taken during a tournament that seems to sum up their relationship and is often used to illustrate their friendship. Ballesteros, the taller of the pair, is standing upright, gazing out over the course. Behind him, Olazábal has leapt into the air, using Ballesteros's shoulders for leverage, to try to get a better view of the action so that for the instant captured in the shot, he actually appears taller than the bigger man. If he had seen further, Olazábal always acknowledged, it was by standing on the shoulders of a giant.

After he had attended the funeral, Olazábal began to think deeply about honouring Ballesteros at the Ryder Cup at Medinah. Not just honouring him, really, but incorporating him into the event, using what Ballesteros stood for in golf and in particular in Ryder Cup competition to inspire his team, somehow making it seem as though he was present just as he had been at every Ryder Cup since 1979.

Ballesteros was too ill to travel to Celtic Manor in 2010 but he did make an emotional call to the European team room the day before play began. Montgomerie, the captain that year, routed the call on to speakerphone so that Ballesteros could address the entire team. There was also a big picture of Ballesteros and Olazábal in the team room in South Wales beneath which the players took their breakfast each day.

'Every one of my team learned what the Ryder Cup meant to Seve when we spoke to him on the eve of the matches,' Montgomerie said later, 'and they will all tell you it was one of the highlights of the week. He fired up the team and we wanted to win it for him.'

Graeme McDowell, the hero of the final day when he sealed the crucial singles victory over Hunter Mahan, was also clear about the emotional impact of Ballesteros's intervention.

'Coming down the final hole,' McDowell said, 'I was thinking about my teammates, I was thinking about Monty and the fans and I was also thinking about Seve. This win is most definitely for him.'

Olazábal recognized that, his own allegiance to his friend aside, Ballesteros was a pivotal figure in the history of both European golf and the Ryder Cup itself. By the mid-1970s, the competition, then contested between the USA and Great Britain and Ireland (who joined the fray in 1971), had become moribund. In the half century from 1927 to 1977, Britain had won only three of the 22 editions of the Ryder Cup. The competition was too one-sided, too predictable and too parochial.

But in 1979, things changed. The British and the Irish players were subsumed into a team representing the European Tour, and the jewel among them was Ballesteros, the young genius who had just won The Open for the first time at Royal Lytham & St Annes at the age of 22.

John Jacobs, the father of the European Tour and the European captain that year at The Greenbrier in White Sulphur Springs, West Virginia, decided that Ballesteros and the only other non-British or Irish member of the team, Antonio Garrido, should play the first Friday morning fourballs match together to symbolize the competition's new beginning.

Ballesteros and Garrido lost to Lanny Wadkins and Larry Nelson and the US went on to win the competition again, but a revolution had begun and Ballesteros led it. He swept all before him. His arrival was as breathtaking and as intoxicating as that of Tiger Woods was to be 20 years later. In 1980 Ballesteros became the first European to win the US Masters.

'Seve was never beaten,' Olazábal told the *Mail on Sunday*'s respected Chief Sports Reporter, Malcolm Folley, a couple of months before Ballesteros died. 'You learn from what you see, and I did that from the way Seve played and the way he acted on the golf course. He broke down barriers.

'He took the concept of golf to a new audience and he opened a lot of doors for European players when he went to the States and won the Masters that first time. We started to believe, as young players, that we could follow in his footsteps. The way he played golf had not been seen before. In his prime, he played from places you weren't supposed to be, yet ended up making a birdie or saving par with some huge shot.'

In a game known for its rules, its reserve and its conventions, Ballesteros was wild and free. There was fire in his belly and the kind of talent in his hands when he wielded a golf club that only comes from above. He was not a safe player. He did not know how to win tournaments easily. He was George Best. He was John McEnroe. Vulnerable sometimes, flawed, too, but always incredibly watchable, always supremely talented.

It would be wrong to say he was golf's first superstar – that was probably Arnold Palmer. But he was European golf's first superstar. That was partly due to his sublime talent, partly due to his looks and his spellbinding charisma and partly due to his unpredictability and his ability to get himself out of trouble. It was a different way of playing golf, a way that said all was not lost if you were not in the middle of the fairway. Ballesteros taught golf about the genius of recovery.

When Phil Mickelson played the shot that won him the Masters for the third time in 2010, a shot clubbed out of the trees to within a few yards of the 13th hole, that was Ballesteros. When Sergio García played the shot for which he is still most famous, from behind a tree at the 1999 PGA Championship at Medinah, that was Ballesteros, too.

He was the man who played The Car Park Shot, after all, one of the most celebrated shots in golf history. That came at the 1979 Open at Royal Lytham & St Annes when he hit his tee shot on the 16th into a temporary parking lot. It came to rest beneath an old Ford Cortina but Ballesteros still managed to make birdie and win his first Claret Jug.

When Ballesteros was diagnosed with a brain tumour in 2008, *The Times'* erudite golf writer John Hopkins composed a warm tribute to him. 'Jack Nicklaus was a straighter driver and Tiger Woods a more prolific winner of major championships,' he wrote, 'and if I had to nominate someone to putt for my life it would be Ben Crenshaw.

'But if I had to put my house on someone getting out of greenside rough, clearing a gaping bunker the other side of which was a flagstick set on a down slope and stopping the ball close enough to sink the ensuing putt, then I would unhesitatingly summon Ballesteros.'

Ballesteros redefined golf's boundaries and shifted its balance of power away from America. In 1985 he was a leading member of the European team that ripped the Ryder Cup out of the hands of the USA for the first time since 1957. And in 1997 he brought his own brand of captaincy to the competition when he led the European side at Valderrama.

He was a phenomenon of manic energy and control-freakery at that Ryder Cup. He was the first coach of a sporting team to ignore the theoretical white lines that divide a manager from the players taking part. Ballesteros captained that European Ryder Cup team from the middle of the fairway, always there on his golf cart, racing from fairway to fairway, cajoling his men, playing every shot.

Ballesteros led his team to a famous victory on the first occasion the Ryder Cup had been hosted outside of Britain or America. He was presented with the trophy by the Infanta Maria, daughter of King Juan Carlos.

'This is my best win ever,' he said. 'I have won five Majors, six Order of Merits, many great tournaments around the world, but I have felt nothing like this. I am the happiest man in the world. This will go down in history because I am the first non-British captain to win the Ryder Cup as a captain and a player. The players in my team played with heart and that is why we won.'

No wonder Olazábal wanted to harness some of the power and emotion that Ballesteros had unleashed on the Ryder Cup. No wonder he wanted to pay tribute to the effect he had had on the evolution of the competition and the contribution he had made to turning it into the greatest, most anticipated, most dramatic event in the golfing calendar.

'I think with José María, you have Seve Ballesteros in terms of a link,' the English golfer, Justin Rose, who was to play such a crucial role at Medinah, said before the competition. 'It's fantastic that José María is the captain. You know that if Seve had been around, he would have been a big part of this team. So it's nice that he is still a big part of this team.'

When the European team got to Medinah, it was obvious Olazábal had not held back. A silhouette of Ballesteros's most famous pose, his clenched-fist salute to the St Andrews' crowd after he had sunk the putt that won The Open in 1984, was branded on the players' sleeves. The inscription '1957–2011' was underneath it to mark the years of his life. And underneath that were five stars, one for each of his Major triumphs.

The clenched fist silhouette was also on each player's golf bag. Ballesteros loved the picture, too. It was tattooed on his left arm and mounted in bronze on the front door of his house in Pedreña. Spanish golf fans refer to the instant of that victory simply as 'El Momento'.

'He always said that was the sweetest moment of his career, winning at St Andrews and making that putt to beat

Tom Watson,' Olazábal said. 'We came up with the idea that it would be nice to have Seve's silhouette, so that every time somebody grabs a club or something from the bag they can see it. I thought it was important to have Seve's memory and presence during this week.

'This was one way that Seve could be with us every step of the way. This is the first Ryder Cup match since he sadly passed away and a fitting tribute to a true champion and a great friend. He has meant a lot to me and the team and I wanted something to make him present for each player. His image will certainly ensure he is alongside us throughout the week.'

But that was not all. When his team went out to play the singles on Sunday, Olazábal decided he wanted them to be wearing navy sweaters, white shirts and navy trousers, the out-fit Ballesteros favoured on the final day of a Major. Davis Love III, the US captain, agreed to the plan even though he had been planning for his team to wear a similar colour scheme. It was as if Olazábal wanted to conjure the spirit of Ballesteros, to see him striding the fairways again, to have another chance to say farewell.

And so Ballesteros came to the aid of his old friend one last time. Olazábal was not everyone's idea of what a Ryder Cup captain should be. He was not a dominant, inspirational, charis-matic leader like Ballesteros had been. Men like Sam Torrance and Colin Montgomerie had followed the Ballesteros template but Olazábal was not like that.

There were concerns about his temperament, too, part-icularly whether he was equipped to deal with the fierce, fierce pressure that being Ryder Cup captain brings. He was vice-captain to Nick Faldo in 2008 when Europe lost to the US at Valhalla and he reacted to the defeat with a startling loss of both his temper and his dignity.

At the post-competition press conference that year in Louisville, Kentucky, Paul Hayward, now the *Daily Telegraph*'s highly respected Chief Sports Writer, asked Faldo a courteously phrased and entirely legitimate question about how hard it would be for him, as one of the great Ryder Cup players, to be saddled with a defeat in his only shot at being Europe's captain.

Before Faldo had a chance to answer, Olazábal jumped in. 'That is not a question that deserves an answer,' he shouted. He became animated and aggressive, railing that it was an unfair question and that Hayward had no right to ask it. He then intimated that perhaps Hayward would like to continue the discussion outside and it was clear by the anger in his voice that he was ready to step up the confrontation.

'I remember that very well,' Olazábal told the *Guardian*'s Donald McRae in a 2011 interview. 'At the time they were putting Nick against the ropes and I think they were being a bit unfair. Nick tried his best and that's why I defended him the way I did. It was the right thing to do. I wasn't really angry. I was just making a point.'

Still, the room was stunned by his behaviour and it brought the press conference to a premature and rather awkward end. When his conduct at Valhalla and the way he had reacted under pressure was brought up two days before the start of play in Medinah, it was clear he was still bristling. Bizarrely, he aimed more criticism at Hayward's question from four years earlier, attempting to insist again that it had somehow been underhand.

This time, Hayward confronted Olazábal after the press conference. He told him the question may have been strongly worded but pointed out that it was by no means unfair. It was a straight question in the aftermath of a tough defeat when no questions are going to be easy. Finally, Olazábal seemed to accept he may have overreacted. The two men shook hands but the whole episode left many wondering how Olazábal would cope as the leader of the team.

The European captain was a strange mix of the passionate and the melancholic. Sometimes, it seems as if he is filled with a great sadness and yet he also has a reputation for being capable of inspiring those around him. He is a single man, a private man. Like Ballesteros did until his death, Olazábal still lives in his birthplace, Fuenterrabia, on Spain's north-west coast.

'Obviously he's made a lot of money, but he leads a simple life,' his one-time caddie Dave Renwick said. 'When I worked for him, he just lived for golf. His only other hobby seemed to be hunting. He enjoys going shooting in the hills with his dogs. That was his life: golf and hunting. He was the most determined player I ever saw.'

Olazábal is also widely respected by his peers. When the time came to choose Europe's 2012 Ryder Cup captain, there was barely a discussion. Everyone knew Olazábal was a candidate and that meant automatically there would be no viable challenger. Thomas Bjørn, the chairman of the European Tour's tournament committee, called the other members to ask their opinions. 'It was unanimous,' he said. Olazábal was the only captain chosen without the need for a meeting.

Some of that respect was earned through Olazábal's cour- ageous fight against rheumatoid arthritis, which has afflicted him through much of his career. There was a time when he feared he would spend the rest of his life in a wheelchair. One of his darkest memories is of being in so much pain that he had to crawl across the floor of his house to get to the toilet.

But Olazábal is a fighter, too. That's what most golfers see in him. Someone with a vital inner strength and a core of determination. That, in turn, was what Olazábal revered about

Ballesteros. 'Every Ryder Cup with Seve was special,' Olazábal told McRae. 'I am fortunate to have lived those moments with him. Certain shots he played, the way he always fought. It sticks in my mind because it's so impressive to see a man giving his best with every shot. I never saw that in any other player.'

As Europe's attempt to retain the Ryder Cup in 2008 slipped away under Faldo's failing leadership, it was Olazábal who stepped up to provide a rousing speech on the Saturday night. Graeme McDowell remembered it as one of the highlights of the competition.

Paul Casey, who played with Olazábal in the 2006 Ryder Cup at The K Club and was in the 2008 team at Valhalla, was equally impressed with the Spaniard's motivational qualities. 'Ollie's the only man who's ever made me cry in the Ryder Cup. He made speeches at both matches, and I cried both times,' Casey said.

Olazábal was, of course, involved in one of the great controversies of the Ryder Cup when his match with Justin Leonard at Brookline in 1999 was disrupted by members of the American team. When Leonard sank a crucial long putt at the 17th, American players and support staff rushed the green and cavorted in celebration on it, ignoring the fact that Olazábal was still waiting to putt.

It prompted Sam Torrance to deliver his famously scathing line: 'And Tom Lehman calls himself a man of God.' Olazábal did not try to inflame the issue and largely kept his own counsel but it made him think more deeply about the ethics of the competition. He recalled the last time things threatened to get out of hand.

'I think the worst atmosphere that doesn't go with the spirit of the Ryder Cup was at Kiawah [Island, South Carolina] in 1991,' Olazábal said. 'That was the turning point.

Tom Watson, the US captain the next time, settled things down. He brought the right spirit back to the match. I don't need to talk to Davis about spirit. He has a lot of respect for the game of golf.'

Olazábal had that going for him, too: he was not Faldo. Faldo had set the bar low when it came to someone for Olazábal to emulate as the last visiting European captain to take on America. Faldo's opening ceremony speech at Valhalla was a festival of cringe, a mixture of dad-at-a-disco comments about one of his players – 'he's single, girls, but only until Sunday' – and embarrassingly inappropriate, desperately un-funny attempted gags such as suggesting Padraig Harrington had 'hit more golf balls than potatoes grown in Ireland'. He also seemed to become confused over whether McDowell was from Ireland or Northern Ireland and then suggested, what the hell, it didn't really matter.

Faldo had rambled on about his daughter's career in fashion and managed to mix up Denmark's Søren Hansen, one of three Scandinavians in his twelve-man team, with Sweden's Henrik Stenson to produce the Nordic composite golfer Søren Stenson. Still, at least he remembered Hansen was there. At Celtic Manor two years later, Corey Pavin introduced his team and forgot about Stewart Cink altogether. At Oakland Hills in 2004, American captain Hal Sutton thanked his wife Ashley for giving him three children whereupon she held up the fingers on her right hand to remind him that, actually, she had given him four.

Say it is nothing to do with the action if you want, but each of those captains seemed to lose the psychological struggle with their opponents early. Olazábal was desperately keen not to make any similar mistakes. He stayed at home in Spain the week before he was to fly to Chicago to work on his speech and check the details of the team arrangements.

'You know me,' he had told McRae the year before. 'I'm a quiet person. But I understand that being Ryder Cup captain is a new scenario. I'll fulfil my duties the best I can but don't expect me to be talking too much. That's the way that I am. I'm not going to try and change it.'

He was keenly aware that, as Lawrence Donegan, the former golf correspondent of the *Guardian* had opined, 'there are no second acts in the life of a Ryder Cup captain these days'. He had one shot at it. He knew the pitfalls. He knew that there would not be a moment where he was not under scrutiny. He knew he had to be on his guard the whole time.

Once again, he had Faldo as a reference point. In the practice rounds at Valhalla, Faldo was photographed with a sheet of paper bearing initials, which looked like his Friday morning foursomes pairings. His attempts to cover up his mistake made him a laughing stock. He said the initials were to remind him about the players' sandwich requests. 'I was simply making sure who wants the tuna, who wants the beef,' Faldo explained to barely suppressed laughter.

It was hardly surprising then that Olazábal chose to adopt a low profile at Medinah, or as low a profile as a team captain can adopt. He chose to take the ego out of the post and leave the headlines to the players. He did not attempt to impose his own personality on the team. He had won two US Masters titles, of course, but he did not talk about that. When he wanted to inspire his players, he turned to the spectre of Ballesteros.

His approach harked back to another time, a time of greater innocence, a time when players were less concerned with their own celebrity, a time which Hayward had referred to when he wrote about the funeral of Ballesteros. 'Much of the woe expressed yesterday,' he said, 'stemmed from people re-connecting with those more innocent times.' In that respect, Olazábal had kept the flame burning with great honour.

There were times as the competition unfolded at Medinah when people began to ask where Olazábal was. He was not the highly visible, hyperactive presence that Montgomerie had been at Celtic Manor. The television cameras did not find him crouching by every tee or sitting on his golf buggy near every green. That was not his style.

Olazábal preferred a low-key approach. He did not want to be up front and centre. He wanted to patrol the margins instead and leave the players to do their work and make their shots. He trusted them. He did not feel the need to micro-manage each of the foursomes and fourballs, morning and afternoon. He stood back and watched. He worked on his pairings.

In many ways, he was the opposite of Montgomerie and Ballesteros as captain. He chose the shadows, not the limelight. Some felt disconcerted by the contrast. That included plenty of members of the press and Montgomerie himself, who, as part of Sky's commentary team at Medinah, amused viewers by referring repeatedly to his status as a winning Ryder Cup captain and generally glorifying his role.

Olazábal would never have done that. There were times over the weekend when his captaincy was described as 'flat' and 'invisible'. There were times when people doubted him. There were times when they wondered if maybe Europe had made the wrong choice. Olazábal did not change. He did not panic. He remained steady and true. The images of Ballesteros were all around him. He knew that, even in death, his old friend could still make the difference.

1

Captain Love and
the new Americans

The first time Davis Love III played in the Ryder Cup, in 1993, he found himself standing on the 18th fairway at The Belfry near the end of his singles match with Costantino Rocca so racked with nerves that he thought he was going to be sick. As he waited for Rocca to play, he wanted to bend over, put his hands on his knees and take breath after deep breath to try to avoid throwing up.

Love had been one hole down with two to play in a match that it had become obvious the US had to win if they were to retain the trophy. All afternoon, Love had studied the leaderboards around the course in one of the rites the competition brings, hoping for more numbers in US red to start replacing European blue.

But now he realized it was all down to him. He had levelled the match at the 17th and then Rocca had carved his tee shot at the 18th deep into the rough to the right of the fairway. Love, a man who has always exuded the easy confidence of a comfortable, loving upbringing, a man full of grace and dignity, a man who nobody dislikes, was suddenly a mess of emotions.

He told himself not to search for his wife, Robin, or his mother, among the galleries. He was worried it might make him start to think about his father, Davis Love Jr, who had been killed in a plane crash near Jacksonville five years earlier. The last time the two men had seen each other, a few hours before his death, his father had talked about how best his son might be able to fulfil his potential. It was a memory that drove Love on in his career. His book, *Every Shot I Take*, was dedicated to his father.

His father had been a fine golfer, too, and an even better coach. Love's younger brother, Mark, was the more talented of the two sons but he was also the more impatient. Davis had a more even temperament. When he could not master a shot, Mark gave up after 15 swings. When the same thing happened to Davis, he persevered until he got it right.

'Dad always told both of us that if he had had our natural talent, he would have been a star,' Love told John Feinstein for his brilliant book *A Good Walk Spoiled*. 'His talent was for work. He always talked about hitting balls until his hands bled when he was a kid. Some days, I would go out and hit all these balls and I'd say "Dad, when will my hands start to bleed?" And he would just look at me and say, "Not for a long time yet."'

As he stood over his ball on the 18th fairway, Love reasoned that allowing his mind to wander on to his lost relationship with his father now might destroy his ability to play the next shot altogether. In the end, he managed to find the edge of the green with his approach and some minutes later, found himself standing on the 18th green with a six-foot putt to retain the Ryder Cup. He could sense that his teammates could barely breathe by this stage. He backed off the putt once, which made the tension even worse. Then he stepped up again and drilled it into the middle of the hole.

He was submerged in a mass of celebrating teammates and it was only after the initial surge of emotion had subsided that he realized he had not shaken hands with Rocca. The Italian had waited for him for a while before giving up and wandering back towards the clubhouse with his wife. Love sprinted after him and when Rocca turned round, Love could see tears in his eyes. 'I hope you're proud of the way you played,' Love told him. 'And I hope your country's proud of you. It should be.' The two men shook hands and hugged each other.

When Love recalled these scenes, he admitted that until he had played in the Ryder Cup, he felt sceptical about the aura that had grown up around it. He had doubted those who told him that the competition was like nothing else in golf. He had not believed them when they said he would be more nervous at the Ryder Cup than he had ever been playing a Major. He had not thought it would be anything special.

'Remember one thing,' Tom Kite had told him about the magic that grips the competition. 'If they've got a sixty-foot putt, expect them to make it. If they're in an unplayable spot, figure they'll find a play. If you're sure we've won a hole, flush the thought. Things are going to happen you've never seen happen before in your entire life.'

Tom Watson, the US captain that year, told Love it was the only event in the world that would make his legs shake when he was trying to take a shot. Love didn't believe him, either. Until, that is, he was making his way to the first tee on Friday morning to play with Kite against Olazábal and Ballesteros in the foursomes. He started to try to persuade Kite to change the plan that Love should be the one to drive off the first tee. Kite smiled and told him they were sticking with the plan. That was when Love felt his legs begin to shake.

'All of a sudden,' Love said, 'it hit me just how big a deal this really was. It wasn't as if I hadn't known it before. But watching on television, just rooting for the US, is an entirely different thing. I mean, there were thousands of people there and, unlike at a tournament, they were going to be watching just four matches and I was going to be playing in one of them.'

Love also recalled that Ballesteros was notorious for his gamesmanship among the American players. By the time Medinah came around, Ballesteros had practically been beatified by Olazábal but Love told an anecdote about how he had been presented with a box of lozenges before that first foursomes match in 1993. He was urged to offer one to Ballesteros the first time Seve coughed just as Love or Kite was about to take an important shot.

It never got to that point but when Love arrived at Medinah with his team, he had just as fierce an appreciation as Olazábal of what makes the Ryder Cup unique in golf. He knew that the pressure of delivering a victory for a group of teammates you respect and admire, the pressure of delivering a victory for your country, is a lot more intense that playing to collect a cheque.

He knew that that particularly applied to men in his team like Bubba Watson and Keegan Bradley, who were nationalistic to the point of going misty-eyed when there was even a mention of the military. And he knew that they were about to find out, just as he had done back at The Belfry, why there is something about the Ryder Cup that makes it stand alone in golf.

The debate about the place the heroes of the competition command in the golfing pantheon rages every time it is played. Is excelling at the Ryder Cup the equivalent of winning a Major? Is it better than winning a Major because you have done it for your team and your country not just yourself? Or is success in the Ryder Cup coupled with failure in Majors — the

Colin Montgomerie Syndrome – an indictment of a player, a tacit acknowledgement he has the talent to beat the best, just not the courage and the will to do it on his own?

In almost every other week of the two years that follow every Ryder Cup, golf will return to being a particularly individual, solitary sport. It's not about the team. It's about being selfish. It's about relying on yourself, on your own mental strength. It's about holding your nerve when you know there's no one there to help you, no one else to rely on, nobody who is going to rescue you if you make a mistake, nobody who is going to play a better ball if you stick your approach in the water.

It is true that when history judges great golfers, it looks at their stroke play record first. It judges them on Majors won rather than how they have performed playing for the USA or Europe. It judges them not on whether they have inspired teammates at Valhalla or Celtic Manor but whether they had the guts to get the job done at Augusta or St Andrews. Woods is judged primarily on the fact that he has won 14 Majors. The fact he has a poor Ryder Cup record is a footnote.

So Woods feels on safe ground when he praises Montgomerie and Ian Poulter, who was the star of the British team at Valhalla, for being great Ryder Cup players. Because there is a subtext there, too. The insinuation is that they might be able to thrive in a team environment but they are not mentally strong enough to excel on their own. It is easy to detect in Woods' words a disdain for those who reach their career highlights in the Ryder Cup.

But Woods is missing something. There is a magical quality to the Ryder Cup that his singularly calculating, ruthlessly selfish mind is unable to process. Anyone who has attended The Open or the US Masters multiple times knows that the Majors can produce fantastic drama and compelling storylines. They are the framework over which a golfer builds his greatness.

But anyone who has also attended multiple Ryder Cups knows that the drama that the competition produces time after time after time beats everything else in golf and most other things in sport. It succeeds spectacularly as a team event in an individual sport in a way that the Davis Cup in tennis, for example, does not. If the Majors are the gauge of individual greatness, the Ryder Cup is the measure of sustained drama at a sporting event.

Why? Because it is so intense. Because it brings 24 of the world's best players together and asks them to play up to five matches in three days. Because it forces fierce rivals like Woods and Mickelson to call a truce and play nice for 72 hours. Because it plays on the best of the old sporting enmity between Europe and the US, the old world and the new.

Because it is increasingly evenly matched and unremittingly tense. Because it is about personalities as well as talent. Because it has the same feel the FA Cup used to have when everyone valued playing in the final as much as or more than winning the league title. Because it allows magnetic personalities like Poulter to have their day against masters of the universe like Woods. Because underdogs can shine in a way they rarely do at a Major. Because Phillip Price can beat Mickelson in the singles at The Belfry in 2002.

And because it is about the team. Because it is about more than an individual, like it is at the Majors. Because the team ethic excites something primitive in sports fans. It allows them to unite in favour of a group and, just as importantly, unite against a group. It plays on American nationalism but one of its greatest triumphs has been to graft mainland Europe on to a Great Britain and Ireland team without diluting the partisan nature of the event.

Ballesteros had plenty to do with that as well. When Europe first became part of the format, it was Ballesteros who led the way. And Ballesteros was so universally popular that his presence sluiced away any misgivings there may have been about widening the talent pool to turn the Ryder Cup into a competitive event again.

His passion was important, too. The manic competitiveness that the intensely combative Ballesteros carried into the event made sure that the new format caught fire and captured the imagination of golf fans on both sides of the Atlantic. As golf grew and grew in popularity in the 1990s, the Ryder Cup was perfectly placed to ride the wave.

The competition seemed to be more keenly anticipated every time it came around. Fuelled by the fervour that surrounded the nail-bitingly close finish at Celtic Manor, the build-up to Medinah was a case in point. In Britain, the Ryder Cup was billed as the perfect ending to the best summer of sport the nation had ever had. It might have been taking place in autumn but, spiritually, it belonged to the epic happenings at the Champions League final, the Tour de France, the Olympics, the Paralympics and the US Open tennis.

English newspapers sent their own teams over in force. The *Daily Telegraph* sent four reporters, the *Daily Mail* sent four. *The Times* had five reporters there. Even in this year of years, there was an expectation that the Ryder Cup would produce something special, something memorable, something moment-ous, something to match everything that had gone before. Why? Because it always did.

No one thought that it could throw up an individual whose feats could match the rest of the heroes of the summer like Jessica Ennis, Mo Farah, David Weir, Ellie Simmonds, Bradley Wiggins and Andy Murray. But as Tom Kite had said to Love, it does not pay to underestimate the melodrama that the Ryder Cup routinely produces.

With Love as captain – he was referred to as Captain Love by the American players and TV networks at Medinah – there was little chance of the competition descending into the ugliness that had disfigured it at Brookline in 1999 and Kiawah Island eight years before when Corey Pavin had worn military fatigues and the US had done its best to turn a golf tournament into an analogy for war.

Love had a kinder, gentler view of the competition. He was a fierce competitor, of course. No one gets to the very top of professional sport without being that and Love had joined the select band of golfers who have won a Major with his victory in the US PGA tournament at Winged Foot in 1997. But he had a sense of perspective that helped him put sport in its place.

'Ryder Cup golf really is about bringing people together,' Love said. 'I played on my first team in 1993, and my wife, Robin, remembers when a Ryder Cup team was much smaller than it is today, with fewer assistants and fewer PGA officials. This year at Medinah, she had the inspired idea to have one giant table in the team room for our first night so that the entire team – the players, assistants, officials and wives – would all be in the same place, doing the same thing.

'Robin did the seating and I sat with Keegan Bradley's girlfriend, Jillian Stacey. I had never really spent any time with her. She's a smart young woman who was suddenly thrust into the middle of golf's most intense week, and she was enjoying it. It was a pleasure getting to know her.'

There were some in America, in fact, who actually felt Love was too nice to be their Ryder Cup captain. Nice is often seen as a weakness in sport. Nice equals vulnerability. Nice equals mental fragility. Nice is bad. Nasty is good. In the debate over Love, many pointed out that two of the best Ryder Cup captains of recent times, Ballesteros and Paul Azinger, were also among the most combative, confrontational golfers on the circuit.

In the States, a public row broke out between two of the country's foremost writers on golf over the issue. It started a few weeks before the competition when *Golf* magazine's senior writer, Cameron Morfit, criticized Love's leadership style, comparing it unfavourably to that of Azinger at Valhalla in 2008 and predicting a US defeat at Medinah.

'Nothing that Love has said or done has seemed all that daring or inspiring,' Morfit wrote. 'What's most worrisome about this year's US side is the decided lack of edginess at the top. Love is a very nice guy, and his highest profile assistant, Fred Couples, routinely comes out on top on those polls about which fellow Tour player you'd most like to go bowling with.'

Morfit was also critical of Love's plan to include basketball legend Michael Jordan in the team's plans, even though Jordan won his six NBA titles with the Chicago Bulls and is a golf fanatic revered by most professional sportsmen everywhere. Morfit questioned what benefit Jordan's presence could bring and pointed out he had also been a prominent presence at the 2004 Ryder Cup at Oakland Hills which was a humiliation for the US.

'On the off-chance that his mere presence will dredge up that awful memory,' Morfit wrote, 'Jordan's invitation to the US team room ought to be rescinded . . . If you believe a Ryder Cup team takes its cues from the captain, whose job it is to convey urgency and fight while deftly managing personalities, then you have to believe Europe is already 1 up, at least.'

But Morfit's article prompted a furious response from Michael Bamberger, the highly respected *Sports Illustrated* columnist, who had also been the ghost-writer for *Every Shot I Take*

15 years earlier. Bamberger, who had remained close to Love, wrote an open letter to Morfit ridiculing his stance, dismissing his arguments and lionizing the American captain. Davis, Bamberger argued in his response, had been chosen to be the Ryder Cup captain for two reasons: that the PGA of America 'think he can lead a team that will win the Cup', and that he 'represents the PGA, and golf itself, in exactly the right way.' Bamberger went on to say that 'this can be summarized in a sentence: Davis believes that golf without good manners is not golf at all. An ill-mannered Ryder Cup violates the spirit of the Ryder Cup.'

Bamberger was right about Love: he was determined that the competition should be played in the right spirit and he never wavered from that in the build-up. He would not be swayed by those who complained he was not being inflammatory enough. 'It's not a war, it's a party,' Love said. 'Do we want to pummel them? Of course. But it's a golf match. We will get chippy but it will be respectful.'

Love stayed true to his word. He had made tentative plans for the US team to wear blue on the final day of the competition but when Olazábal made him aware that he had been hoping to dress his players in blue to honour the memory of Ballesteros, Love, as gracious as ever, said he was happy to choose a different colour scheme for his side.

Even at an event as partisan as the Ryder Cup, it was difficult for the Europeans to do anything but admire Love. Most of them knew him and liked him anyway. Everybody who knows him seems to like him. He's the guy who thanks the kid who's carried the scoreboard at the end of every round. He's the guy who always stops to talk to reporters, good day or bad day, and is never rude. He's the guy who always tips the locker-room attendant at tournaments.

Sure, there were isolated moments in the build-up when things were said that ought not to have been said. But the build-up is long, laborious and exhaustive. The captains do their first interviews on the Monday before the competition starts and then on every day subsequently until it ends. Most of the players do at least two comprehensive interviews on the stage in the marquee that houses the Media Centre.

Somebody is going to say something that might rile the other side slightly, intentionally or not. There were a couple of flashpoints at Medinah but nothing to compare with many of the incidents in the past. At Love's Ryder Cup debut at The Belfry, for instance, there was an almighty row when Tom Watson ordered his team not to sign any autographs at the pre-match dinner. Watson even refused to sign a menu for Sam Torrance, who flew into a huff. The English newspapers made a meal of it the next day. 'Fork Off', one headline said.

The closest there got to anything like that before Medinah was when Poulter said in his Media Centre interview that sometimes he felt like he wanted to kill the opposition during the Ryder Cup. But no one took offence. It was part of the rhetoric of the event. One of the American players said something similar soon afterwards. It was all quickly forgotten.

There was no appetite for a conflagration. Love was not the type to try to incite the crowd or wind his players up into a frenzy. He was way too decent for any proper attempt at gamesmanship. Love hinted that the atmosphere at Medinah, packed full with Chicago sports supporters who have a reputation for being both raucous and fanatical, might unsettle the European players. He said they would probably have never heard anything like it before. But that was as far as he went.

'I go back to what Tom Watson said about the Ryder Cup,' Love said. 'It's an adventure. It's not just a three-day golf match. You build relationships in this event that you don't build anywhere else; friendships, respect for your competitors that you don't gain in a regular tournament. José María Olazábal is right, too. There will be moments that happen out there that only happen in a Ryder Cup in that kind of pressure. These guys are going to have moments out there this week that will change their careers and that they will remember the rest of their lives.'

2 Big hitting, freewheeling . . . but no rough stuff

The competition was to begin at the Medinah Country Club Course Number 3 on Friday 28 September. José María Olazábal arrived in Chicago four days earlier, touching down at the city's Rockford Airport, flanked by vice-captains Darren Clarke and Miguel Ángel Jiménez and clutching the 17-inch-high gold trophy that was soon to become the object of another epic struggle between the USA and Europe. Europe had won it four of the last five times it had been staged.

There were no pictures of the team standing on the steps of the aircraft on arrival. Only three players – Francesco Molinari, Nicolas Colsaerts and Paul Lawrie – travelled with him on the charter flight from London. The rest journeyed there from their homes in the US, particularly the colony of British golfers that has sprung up around Lake Nona in Florida. Some speculated Europe's celebrated team spirit would be diluted as a result.

There was much talk about the hostility that the European team would face at Medinah. There was going to be something special about the level of support for the home team, everyone agreed. Chicago is one of America's great sports centres, full of tradition and history. Luke Donald, one of the European team, had settled in Chicago and said he would begin any visitor's tour of the city at Wrigley Field, the ivy-clad home of the Chicago Cubs baseball team. The city is also home to a more successful baseball franchise, the White Sox, to the Chicago Bears NFL team, the Blackhawks of the NHL and, of course, the Chicago Bulls basketball team who dominated the NBA in the 1990s with a team led by the great Michael Jordan and Scottie Pippen.

There were a few scare stories about the intimidation the European team might face. But that was nothing new. The reality is that the atmosphere is much the same for European golfers at a US Ryder Cup as it is for the US players when the event is staged in Europe. It is loud and it is partisan but after the lows of Brookline in 1999 when Colin Montgomerie was subjected to such appalling abuse that his father walked off the course, much had changed for the better.

Montgomerie aired concerns that the situation might have regressed, that what he saw as a post-9/11 truce might have lapsed with the passage of time. But Olazábal and the European players were unconcerned. They accepted that the support of the crowd was part of the occasion, part of what made the Ryder Cup a unique event in their sport. They did not seek to make it an issue.

Most believed the competition would be desperately close. Nick Faldo, the losing captain at Valhalla in 2008, predicted a tie, which would, of course, be enough for Europe to retain the trophy. The consensus was that they were two of the strongest, most evenly matched teams ever assembled. Viewers were told to prepare themselves for a nail-biter.

The ten players who qualified automatically for Europe were Rory McIlroy, Justin Rose, Paul Lawrie, Graeme McDowell, Francesco Molinari, Luke Donald, Lee Westwood, Sergio García, Peter Hanson and Martin Kaymer. Four of those players – Kaymer, Donald, Westwood and McIlroy – had held the position of world number one at some point over the previous 18 months.

The speculation over the captain's two wild card picks was not as frenzied as usual but there was still plenty of potential for controversy. Being selected for, or omitted from, a Ryder Cup team is still one of the seminal moments of a player's career and there have been occasions where a captain's decision has been met with undisguised fury by the man on the wrong end of it.

Thomas Bjørn, one of Olazábal's assistant captains at Medinah, was left out of Europe's 2006 Ryder Cup team by Ian Woosnam, who chose Lee Westwood instead. Westwood was below Bjørn in the rankings but had won at the K Club, the venue for the competition that year, in the past. Woosnam broke the news to Bjørn in a hotel bar. Bjørn did not take it well.

'I'm shocked and have totally lost respect for Ian Woosnam,' he said. 'My relationship with him is completely dead. It looks like he needs to learn how to be a captain. If the choice had been made only on competitive results, I could go along with it. But I'm in front of Lee in all the rankings, I have played better than him in the qualifying phase and then Woosnam bases his decisions on results which are more than five years old.

'I don't understand the way he is handling the situation. I hadn't heard from him for six months. I have spoken to several of the players who are in the team and they haven't heard a word from Woosnam either. To be captain and not even communicate with your team at all – it doesn't give you much respect. He came into the bar at the hotel and gave me 20 seconds about Lee having won twice at the K Club. In a bar. That kind of sums it up.'

Woosnam's response was the only one that really mattered. He led Europe to a record 18½ – 9½ victory.

Olazábal did not have any dilemmas of that magnitude. It was widely accepted that he would hand one of the wild cards to Ian Poulter, who not only had a magnificent Ryder Cup record that included an unbeaten run in singles matches, but had also recorded victories in high-profile tournaments like the Volvo World Match Play and the WGC-Accenture Match Play.

That left one spot. Most believed the favourite to win it was the longest hitter on the European Tour, Nicolas Colsaerts, who had never played in the Ryder Cup before but had won the World Match Play championship in May 2012 at Casares, in Spain. Olazábal thought Colsaerts' game would suit the course at Medinah, which had been set up to favour length off the tee ahead of accuracy.

The only potential flashpoint was the candidature of Padraig Harrington, a three-time Major winner and a veteran of six Ryder Cups. Whatever his form, it would be a big call leaving out a man of his stature for a Belgian rookie. Harrington is a popular figure in European golf and even though he had endured a poor run, men like former Ryder Cup skipper Bernard Gallacher were convinced he should get the last wild card pick ahead of Colsaerts.

But there was another issue. Olazábal and Harrington were not friends. A once cordial relationship had been ruined when they played each other in a Seve Trophy match at El Saler, near Valencia, in 2003. The two men were involved in a pivotal final-day singles match, and on the third hole Harrington asked a referee for a ruling on whether Olazábal was entitled to repair two pitch marks on his putting line.

While Harrington waited for the official, Olazábal made the repairs anyway. Harrington made a sarcastic comment about Olazábal's 'gardening' and even though the Irishman insisted he wasn't impugning Olazábal's honour, the Spaniard angrily picked up his ball, conceded the hole, stormed to the next tee and played the rest of the match in silence.

Harrington halved the match to help Great Britain and Ireland retain the trophy.

A heated discussion between Harrington and Olazábal ensued right after the match and, when Harrington emerged, he said, 'It's not worth losing a friend over, but we had fifteen very awkward holes. I was not trying to question his integrity, but that's what he thought and I can ten per cent see his side.''

The relationship was never the same after that. Some, in fact, described their subsequent attitude to each other as 'a feud'. Harrington knew that, when he failed to qualify automatically, his chance had probably gone. Sure enough, on the eve of the public announcement of the wild card picks, he got the call from Olazábal. 'He was nineteenth on the list of players,' the captain said curtly the next day, 'and that was a little bit too far down. He took it well.' Colsaerts became the first Belgian to be selected for the Ryder Cup.

The American side they were facing was also high on quality and experience although none of the eight players with Ryder Cup experience had a winning record in the competition. In their favour, one of the rookies who made the team, Webb Simpson, was the reigning US Open champion while Bubba Watson, with only one appearance to his name, had won the 2012 US Masters.

Love had tough decisions to make with his captain's picks,

too. The American system allocated four spots as captain's choices and most assumed that Steve Stricker and Jim Furyk would be two of them. Love rated Stricker as the most consistent player on the tour over the last five years. He was also the man Woods was said to enjoy playing with most.

Furyk, who had played in the last seven Ryder Cups, had had a difficult year and had blown a lead in the US Open but was still regarded as vital for his experience and record in team play. He had won five points out of five for the US at the Presidents Cup in 2011 and Love wanted him because he believed he could pair him with anybody on the team. 'I need Jim Furyk,' Love said. 'I need Steve Stricker. All of the guys on the team will benefit from those guys being in the team room, being in the locker room.'

The third of the four captain's spots was claimed by Dustin Johnson. Johnson was one of the biggest hitters on the tour and Medinah, at 7,657 yards long, was ideally suited to his game. Johnson had come into form at exactly the right time, too. 'I know I'm going to love watching Dustin round here,' Love said at Medinah.

That left one more pick. The outsider was Ricky Fowler, the charismatic, flamboyant young player who had provided a memorable cameo at Celtic Manor by winning the last four holes of his singles game with Edoardo Molinari to halve the match and keep America's slim hopes alive. Fowler was still regarded as one of the brightest hopes for American golf and had beaten Rory McIlroy in a play-off to win at Quail Hollow in May. But he had not finished higher than a tie for 24th in any of his last six events and his hopes had faded.

Many hoped that Love would give his last pick to Hunter Mahan. The Texan had only just missed out on automatic selection, finishing ninth in the US rankings, and there were sentimental reasons for picking him, too. It was Mahan, two years earlier at Celtic Manor, who had asked for the responsibility of playing in the final game of the singles and found himself up against Graeme McDowell.

The US had mounted a superb comeback in the rain-blighted event and Mahan knew that if he could halve his match with the Northern Irishman, the competition would be a 14–14 draw and the US would retain the Ryder Cup. But he was two down going to the 17th and when he fluffed a chip on the edge of the green and then missed a long putt, Mahan conceded the match and handed the Ryder Cup back to Europe.

Mahan had been inconsolable afterwards. He had attended the post-match press conference with the rest of the team but was clearly struggling to keep his emotions in check. When he was asked about his match, he gave in to his anguish. 'He just beat me today,' Mahan said, his voice quivering. They were the only words he could muster.

Next to him, Phil Mickelson put an arm around his shoulder and seeing that Mahan was overcome, answered several questions for him. Other teammates praised him, too. They talked about his courage and shifted the blame to other moments where a point had been lost. Mahan kept rubbing his eyes, desperately trying not to break down.

'I'm just proud to be a part of this team,' Mahan managed to say at one stage. 'It's a close team, and . . .'

Then Mahan faltered again and Mickelson gave him an affectionate slap on the shoulder. 'We are all proud to be part of this team,' Mickelson said. 'We came within half a point. But we could look anywhere throughout those twenty-eight points for that half a point.'

But, like Fowler, Mahan was also struggling for form. He had won twice earlier in the season, including the WGC-

Accenture Match Play Championship where he beat McIlroy, but had one top-ten finish since winning in Houston on April Fool's Day. He missed the cut in two of the last three events before Love announced his decision and finished among the also-rans in the other.

Mahan clung to the hope that he might still sneak into the team and made no secret of the fact that he was desperate to redeem himself for what had happened in South Wales. But when the call came, Love told him he had not made it. He had gone for the rookie, Brandt Snedeker, instead.

'No one would ever accuse Love, one of the game's good guys, of playing favorites,' Feinstein wrote on his golfchannel.com blog, 'but it's worth pointing out that Snedeker and Love are both represented by the same company. Snedeker is also part of what is known on Tour as the "Sea Island mafia", players like Love, Snedeker, Zach Johnson, Matt Kuchar and Jonathan Byrd who all live in Sea Island, Georgia.'

Everybody felt for Mahan. 'I just feel empty right now,' he said when he arrived at Crooked Stick Country Club for the BMW Championship, the first event after the announcement. 'I felt like I wanted to redeem myself somewhat because you feel somewhat responsible. It hurt at the moment it happened. It was one of those things where it's an emotional week.

'It's probably the most emotional week you'll have as a player, just because of the energy the crowd brings, from a positive and negative perspective. It's one of those things that seems to last longer inside of you than just one tournament. But I just didn't play good enough to make the team. And that's okay. It's okay to get beat by somebody. That's part of golf, and that's part of the game.'

Despite their losing records, the men who qualified automatically for the US team made a formidable line-up. Woods,

Watson, Jason Dufner, Keegan Bradley, Simpson, Zach Johnson, Matt Kuchar and Phil Mickelson topped the rankings. Of the top 17 ranked players in the world, 11 were on the American team. And six of Europe's players were ranked below the lowest American, Furyk, who was number 23.

As for Snedeker, the news about making the team seemed to have a positive effect on his game. The weekend before the Ryder Cup, he won the Tour Championship in Atlanta, at which he also clinched the FedEx Cup play-offs title and won a combined pay cheque of $11.44m.

'I made my picks based on pairings,' Love said. 'I want them to be clear before they get there who they'll play with in the practice rounds and in the matches. There won't be any lobby-ing about playing with certain guys come Monday night of Ryder Cup week. There will be no question marks. It can change during the week, of course, but who you see practising together in the Tuesday round will have been decided the week before.

'That comes from the success Paul Azinger had at Valhalla in 2008 and from what Fred Couples has done as captain in the Presidents Cup. The more I think about it, the more I realize that this is like being a football coach. In football you need to have your players ready before the game. It's the same thing with the Ryder Cup.

'As fun as it was to break the news to those four, it was just as difficult to tell the others they didn't make it. I've been around those guys a long time and that wasn't fun at all. Plus, once the Ryder Cup ends, it's not like I can go duck and hide on the Champions Tour. I'm headed right back out on the PGA Tour to play the end of the season and I'll be playing with these guys again, probably even paired with them. I'll have to face them.'

Michael Bamberger, who was planning to speak to Love

every day during the competition, leapt to his defence once more over the picks. 'Making his four captain's picks was surely agonizing for him,' he wrote, 'but his choices were really solid: Jim Furyk, who will likely only play three times, but will come to play in each of those sessions; Steve Stricker, who will likely play with Tiger four times and has proven himself to be a crucial part of that formidable team; Brandt Snedeker, who has a great disposition and the ability to keep his putting stroke on line under pressure; and Dustin Johnson, who has more pure jock in him than pretty much anybody in the game today. His picks made the team – the TEAM – better. They have to be looked at collectively.'

Medinah looked like heaven during the last week of September. The weather defied the forecasts. The sun shone every day. The air was crisp and cool. Some of those walking the course said that the Midwest in the Fall was America at its most beautiful. The course enhanced that impression. Its fairways were lined by majestic oaks, the colours of the leaves growing more vivid with every day of autumn's advance, and the waters of Lake Kadijah glinting in the bright light.

The club had hosted the US Open three times and the PGA twice, in 1999 and 2006. Woods had won the PGA both times. It was also the course where a 19-year-old Sergio García had played his famous shot from behind an oak tree on the 16th in 1999 as he chased Woods all the way home. Some of the visitors to the Ryder Cup went looking for the tree only to find it had been felled when it fell victim to disease.

'Yeah, it lived its full life, but it was dead, unfortunately. It was a safety hazard, so we had to take it down,' said Curtis Tyrrell, Medinah's director of golf course operations. More than 400 oaks had been cut down on the course for the same reason. The club had also spent more than $1m on a greens renovation project that included a radical redesign of the 15th hole. The other startlingly obvious feature was that there was no rough.

'I struggled for two years to come up with a way to get an advantage,' Love, one of the game's original big-hitters, said. 'We have twenty-four of the best players in the world here and they are all pretty good at adapting to conditions but one thing I've never liked is rough. I've been lucky enough to have a little bit of an influence on two golf tournaments, the McGladrey Classic that I host in Georgia and this Ryder Cup, and neither one of them had a lot of rough. I just don't like rough.

'I think the fans want to see a little excitement. They want to see birdies. Valhalla was exciting. There were a lot of birdies. Even holes tied at birdies are more fun than six-footers tying for par. We want to let these unbelievable athletes freewheel it a little bit and play. You know, you're not going to trick them by all of a sudden having deep grass. But we're a long-hitting, freewheeling, fun-to-watch team and this course should play to our strengths.'

The combination of the lack of rough and the tree-felling operation added to the impression that Medinah was going to be wide open. It might still be a disadvantage if a player didn't land his drive on the fairway, but not much of one. It was an invitation to grip it and rip it and not worry too much about the consequences if it wasn't on line.

That was what Love wanted. It played to his instincts. This was a man, after all, who struck the second-longest drive in golf history, a 476-yard drive at the 2004 Mercedes Championships on the wide, wide fairways of the Plantation Course in Hawaii. In Watson and Dustin Johnson, he had two of the top four longest drivers on the PGA Tour (McIlroy was fifth). Watson drove the ball 315 yards on average in the season before Medinah. Johnson was just behind with an average of 306 yards.

Woods was so long off the tee in his youth that Augusta National changed their course to try to tame him for the Masters. And Mickelson and Dufner were also among the longest hitters on the tour, ahead of all the other Europeans except Lee Westwood. Westwood was also deadly accurate off the tee, a trait not always shared by Watson and Mickelson in particular. Like Ballesteros, part of their genius lay in recovery and Medinah was set up for that.

'You're talking about no rough, some of the trees are missing, so you're looking at great golf out of the trees when you hit one wayward,' Watson said. 'Everybody has the ability to hit the shot out of the trees. We're going to see the big hook, the big cuts, over trees, under trees, around bunkers to make birdies. I think it is just made for a spectacular game of golf, no matter what team you're pulling for.'

The Europeans were a little less enthusiastic, particularly Westwood and Sergio García, who compared the set-up unfavourably to the way it had been in 1999. 'There's not a lot of thinking when you get on the tee,' García said at his pre-tournament press conference. 'You can pretty much hit it nice and hard and, even if you miss, pretty much every time you'll have a shot.'

Still, by then the talking was almost over. Three days of interviews in the Media Centre marquee were almost done. There was just enough time for Azinger, who had positioned himself as the guru of American golf since he had captained the US team to victory at Valhalla, to advise Love's men that they had to target McIlroy and take him down.

'The key to this whole Ryder Cup is Rory McIlroy,' Azinger said. 'If we can beat Rory, we win this Ryder Cup. Just like we used to do with Seve and Europe has done with Tiger, the USA has to find Rory, figure out what slot he's in, either teaming up with Graeme McDowell or in singles, and put our hottest players against him.'

Woods also enjoyed trying to crank up the pressure on McIlroy a little. He said his successor as world number one would have to deal with the pressure. 'It's part of being consistent,' he said. 'You're always going to want to try and take out their best player, and that's just part of the deal. That's a fun challenge. I certainly have relished it over the years and I'm sure he's going to relish it this week.'

When McIlroy appeared for his press conference, journalists asked him about what Woods and Azinger had said. It was noted that he did not smile as he gave his answer, that his customary mask of jaunty amiability slipped as he leaned closer to the microphone. 'Whoever wants to take me on, they can take me on,' he said.

Finally, on Thursday evening, the two teams and their wives and girlfriends convened for the Opening Ceremony. The pop star-turned-actor Justin Timberlake read a poem called 'Golf' which included the line 'golf is as sweet and passionate as your lover on a warm summer's night' and generally plumbed new depths of schmaltz.

Then, Olazábal took the stage. He said he had experienced both great joy and great pain in the Ryder Cup. He paid tribute to Ballesteros. 'Seve, we miss you,' he said. And then he turned to Love and to the Ryder Cup itself as it sat there on a plinth between them. 'I know how much you want this lovely, gold trophy back,' Olazábal said, 'but we have every intention of taking it back home with us.'

3 Rabble-rousing in the Midwest in the fall

On Friday, the players began arriving at Medinah well before dawn. The club was already busy with support staff making last-minute preparations. Spectators were striding down the road from the Metra train stop at Medinah Road a couple of miles away. Coaches were rumbling in from the media hotels 15 minutes to the east in Itasca. Floodlights lit up the paths to the course. Police shouted instructions.

Fans crowded round the first tee in the dark. The grandstand behind it was packed more than 90 minutes before the first match began. Another grandstand, to the right of the tee, was also crammed full. Opposite it, between the tee and the clubhouse, crowds 10 or 15 deep stood patiently in the chill of the early morning, waiting for the action to begin.

Neither captain knows which players or in what order his opposite number has chosen for each session. But just as Azinger had suggested he might, Olazábal had decided to make a statement by sending Rory McIlroy out first. He was the world number one, after all. Olazábal wanted him to get Europe off to a flying start so that his team could hit the front early and silence the crowds a little. He paired him, as expected, with Graeme McDowell, his countryman from Northern Ireland and the hero of the last Ryder Cup at Celtic Manor.

Love had anticipated Olazábal's move. He too had front-loaded his team. He had nominated the lugubrious veteran Jim Furyk and the rookie Brandt Snedeker as his first pair. Love had assumed McIlroy would go out first and he was keenly aware that, the previous weekend in Atlanta, Snedeker had won the last event of the FedEx Cup play-off series, the US PGA Tour Championship, and in the process had pipped McIlroy to the $10m FedEx bonus for topping the play-off points table.

It was a stunning coup for Snedeker. The *Daily Mail*'s golf correspondent, Derek Lawrenson, described it as 'a heist'. Everyone had expected the battle for the $10m bonanza to be a shoot-out between McIlroy and Tiger Woods but Snedeker, an ebullient, breezy 31-year-old from Nashville, Tennessee, had stolen the jackpot away from both of them.

It seemed like early vindication for Love choosing Snedeker as one of his captain's picks. He was in the form of his life, he had the hottest putter in the game and he was brimming with confidence. Furyk, despite blowing a chance to win the US Open in San Francisco a few months earlier, was another captain's pick, a man that Love believed he could rely upon to be a steadying, experienced influence.

The crowd around the first tee was loud and expectant by the time the players walked across the bridge from the practice putting green in front of the clubhouse, which allowed them to bypass the hordes of fans standing to the left of the fairway. There were plenty of European flags but the loudest cheers, inevitably, were for the American team.

The atmosphere was good-natured rather than hostile. For some time before McIlroy, McDowell, Furyk and Snedeker had appeared, American vice-captain Fred Couples had been having fun with the supporters. He had walked out on to the tee and started orchestrating chants from both sides, feigning disappointment at the volume of 'Ole, Ole, Ole' from the European fans and expressing approval at the racket created by American supporters yelling 'USA, USA, USA' over and over again.

At one point, a television producer took it upon himself to walk over to some of the European fans grouped in the grandstand behind the tee and urge them on in their singing. There was no need. The atmosphere was at fever pitch. Helicopters hovered overhead, Darren Clarke ambled on to the tee smoking a cigar and even Furyk, one of the least likely rabble-rousers in Ryder Cup history, leapt off the bottom step of the bridge and strode towards the crowd, his left hand cupped to his ear beneath a beanie hat that made his face look even longer.

The Ryder Cup gets to everyone sooner or later. 'It's golf but not as we know it,' the Sky trailer had told everyone and it was right. It was upon us again and suddenly all the dramas, all the incredible highs and lows it is capable of producing, came flooding back.

The Ryder Cup is like no other event in golf and few other events in sport. Partly, that is because there are moments during it when it seems to turn accepted interpretations of golf on their head. It unleashes emotions in the players and the fans that other golf tournaments do not seem to.

No one who was there, for instance, will ever forget what it was like to be in the crowd around the 17th green at Celtic Manor in 2010. It was more like being at a football match than a golf tournament. McDowell needed to win the last match against Hunter Mahan to regain the Ryder Cup for Europe. Everything was unbelievably tense and the barriers that usually separate fans from their sporting heroes came down.

There were no ropes to separate fans from the field of play any more. Thousands of supporters clustered all around the green, right to the very edges of the putting surface, standing there with European captain Colin Montgomerie as he teetered on the edge of a nervous breakdown. It was wonderful, wonderful chaos. Right there, right then, sitting above the 17th green looking out over the Welsh valleys, it had felt that this was about as good as sport gets.

It had felt like golf, sometimes so sedate and so stuffy, had a capacity for drama that other more breathless sports cannot match. And when poor Mahan fluffed his chip from the edge of the green, missed the following putt and conceded the match, everyone ran on. There was a pitch invasion. At a golf tournament. It was as if the natural order of things had been overturned.

What a time that was. Getting close enough to Monty in the crazy melee to be sprayed in the face by champagne aimed at him. Watching his emotional confusion in the very moment of his greatest victory. Hearing a Welsh voice amid the cacophony of celebration. 'Well done, Monty boy,' it was saying.

Leaving the 17th in a demented conga line of players, cameramen and journalists and seeing Rory McIlroy in it, too. Strolling down the side of the 18th flecked with mud and happiness and looking back at the army of fans heading down the hill like soldiers following their generals. 'It felt – to hell with it – Shakespearean,' Martin Samuel wrote in a brilliant piece in the *Daily Mail* the following morning.

There was more that day, too. Seeing a golf cart arrive at the 18th green and doing a wheelie, nearly tipping Lee Westwood and Ian Poulter off the back.

Getting caught in another scrum on the 18th when McDowell was interviewed by a television crew and the crowd drowned him out with its chanting.

Sitting in the media tent and seeing the other side of things, watching Mahan, tormented by guilt, break down in tears, sobbing and saying simply: 'He beat me.' Watching Phil Mickelson intervene and take the microphone from Mahan, hearing Mickelson talk about the points he had lost for his team. Realizing that Mickelson was taking the blame for the defeat, that without actually saying it, he was telling Mahan it was not his fault. Realizing everything they say about Mickelson being a classy guy was true.

Thinking it didn't really feel as though anyone had lost the match, that it just felt as though everyone who had played a part in that day was a winner. Riding the bus back up the hill in the darkness, seeing the lights in the clubhouse and the lights in the valleys. Hoping that maybe, before too many years passed, a day like that would come again.

As they went out for their foursomes that morning at Medinah, McDowell and McIlroy, Furyk and Snedeker, that was what they were playing for. That was the glory they were trying to achieve just as it was the fate they were trying to avoid. They knew what was on offer at the end of the three days of competition that stretched ahead. They knew that when it was over, just like at Celtic Manor, they would either be in heaven or in hell.

No wonder McDowell was nervous as he waited to play the first, a 433-yard par four. Everyone had assumed it would be McIlroy who took the first shot for Europe at Medinah. Everybody had assumed that the symbolism of the world's number one striking the first blow would appeal. But instead it was his mate, GMac, who stepped forward, hitched up the sleeves on his lime green top and, as the crowd stilled, launched his drive off the tee.

As opening salvos go, it did not bode well for his team's chances. McDowell hooked his shot so badly that it sliced through the lower branches of one of the giant oaks on the left side of the fairway. A thicket of decapitated twigs fell to the turf. A cluster of yellowing leaves followed them down, incriminating evidence of the ball's trajectory. McDowell grimaced and smiled nervously at McIlroy. Olazábal appeared behind them both at that point, laughing, trying to defuse the tension.

McDowell's drive had come to rest between the marquee housing The Captain's Club II and corporate hospitality tent number 36, which was the entertaining base of the Aeroterm Vanquish Group. It was not quite the start Europe had been hoping for. In fact, as the first shot in a massive sporting event, it was reminiscent of Steve Harmison's opening ball wide in the First Test at the Gabba in 2006. That presaged a desperate Ashes series for England.

The idea that McDowell's tee-shot might also prove to be an enduring symbol of sporting despair lasted for less than a minute. That was how long it took Furyk to address his ball and slam his drive in the same direction as McDowell's. It didn't dislodge any leaves but it came to rest a few yards away from the European pair's ball.

The first hole was halved. The second was even more dramatic. A 192-yard par three that requires a carry over Lake Kadijah, McIlroy left his tee-shot on the fringe of the green, close to a sprinkler cover. When McDowell arrived at the scene, he requested a free drop and even though the rules official accompanying the match agreed, Furyk objected.

Furyk said he did not believe a free drop was legitimate. He said he did not think the sprinkler cover interfered with McDowell's approach to the shot in any way. McDowell was furious. Around the green, the spectators were agog that the competition should have taken a controversial turn so quickly. McDowell refused to back down and there was a long delay while the head referee was called.

'I looked over to see what was happening,' Furyk said. 'I saw that he was going to get relief and get to probably drop the ball into the fringe so they'd be putting rather than chipping. When I looked to see where the ball was, I believe it was a good four inches – I'm probably being conservative – four to five inches ahead of that sprinkler head.

'They were going to gain a big advantage by being able to drop that ball. He had a sticky lie and a very delicate chip and to be able to putt that ball would have been a huge advantage and I really didn't feel in any situation, whether it be match play or medal play, that it could be deemed a drop.

'It created some tension for the rest of the round. As I told Graeme and Rory, "I don't blame you for trying, for asking." Trying is a bad word; I don't blame them for asking. Graeme said: "I thought it was about a fifty–fifty and you're entitled to your opinion."

'I just disagreed with the official and to have the head referee come out and look at it, he didn't really waste a lot of time. He pretty much immediately said that Graeme needed to play the ball as it lies. I'm not trying to incite any tension or bother anyone but it's my job for my teammates and for my team to kind of protect ourselves and the rules.'

Furyk's protection worked. There was ironic applause for the head referee when he finally stepped on to the green after a ten-minute delay to the match. As Furyk said, he decided quickly that McDowell had to play the ball from where it lay. McDowell shrugged. The crowd hollered and hooted. 'Plenty of room,' a voice shouted delightedly.

McDowell clipped his shot six feet past the hole and, after Furyk had played the US's second shot, there was another disagreement about who was closest to the hole. A driver was produced from a bag to try to provide an accurate measurement.

Europe lost that battle, too. McIlroy putted first and slid his putt left. Snedeker stood over his putt and drained it. The USA were 1 up.

McIlroy stalked off the green, his hands buried deep in his pockets, his face like thunder. The crowd roared its delight. 'USA, USA,' they chanted again and again. 'Atta Boy, Jimmy,' another man shouted at Furyk approvingly as he marched towards the third tee. The atmosphere felt ugly. It did not seem to augur well for what lay ahead.

It was not long before the match took another dramatic twist. At the par-four 4th hole, McDowell's approach had shot through the back of the green. McIlroy walked over to inspect the lie, which was about 45 feet from the hole, close to where a small group of English journalists were standing.

The chip that he produced was a thing of almost impossible delicacy and accuracy, a piece of craftsmanship fashioned with breathtaking skill. He lifted it only a few feet off the ground, a little higher and a little longer than a bump and run, and pitched it on the edge of the green, which sloped downwards from back to front.

It seemed for a moment as though the ball would lose momentum and stop but McIlroy had judged it perfectly. It trickled slowly at first but then it picked up pace and rolled swiftly and obediently into the centre of the cup. McIlroy and McDowell celebrated with gusto, leaving no one in any doubt that there was something extra riding on this match after what had happened on the second green. They gave each other a high five and McIlroy whirled his arms, urging the European supporters in the crowd to increase the volume of their support. The match was all square.

Europe went 1 up at the 6th after McIlroy holed an eight-foot putt for birdie, the Americans brought the game level at the 8th and then Europe pulled away. They went 1 up again at the 9th when McDowell nailed a 15-footer for a winning birdie. At the 10th, Furyk banished any lingering suspicion he had been guilty of gamesmanship at the 2nd when he called a penalty shot on himself after his ball moved while he was taking a practice swing. That cost the Americans another hole and put Europe 2 up.

When McIlroy made a 10-foot par putt at the 11th and Snedeker missed the chance to halve the hole, it seemed Europe was on the verge of claiming the emphatic first match victory Olazábal had craved. But at the 13th, a McIlroy chip from the back of the green rolled past the hole and kept rolling. 'See ya later,' an American voice shouted. 'See ya later.'

The Americans dragged themselves back to two down and suddenly they sensed an escape. At the 15th, McDowell tried to drive on to the putting surface over the lake at the front right of the green. 'Get in the water,' a US fan screamed as McDowell's ball flew through the air. The ball obliged. It was not even close to carrying. Furyk smashed his drive on to the edge of the green. 'Way to go, Jimbo,' the great American basketball player, Michael Jordan, muttered as he watched with the media at the edge of the putting surface. It may be the first time Furyk has ever been called Jimbo.

Now the US were only one hole back and that changed at the 16th when Furyk speared his second shot to within a few feet of the hole. The match was all square going to the 17th and all square going to the 18th, too, but all the momentum seemed to be with Furyk and Snedeker.

But then Snedeker cracked. It fell to him to drive at the 18th and he sliced it wildly into the trees. This was the man, don't forget, who had won more than $10m in prize money a few days earlier, the man who had outplayed McIlroy for the biggest money on offer in the game.

But now, as he and Furyk stood on the brink of what would have been a hugely significant victory for the US, he crumbled. His ball came to rest deep in the woods. It left Furyk hemmed in on all sides. There was no scope for a recovery shot on to the green. All that was left for Furyk was to pitch out on to the fairway and hope that the Europeans would fluff their approach.

It didn't happen, although after McDowell had hit his approach into a greenside bunker, America still had a chance to halve the match. But Furyk slid his par putt wide and McDowell, left with a six-foot putt to win the match, drained it and raised his arms aloft.

'It was a great game of golf,' McDowell said afterwards. 'It really personified the Ryder Cup this morning. We played some great golf to be 3 up and two very gutsy players come back at us with a few birdies and we're playing these last two holes all square and having to hit some quality shots down the stretch.'

And then, as he stood there on the 18th green and the television cameras moved away to another interviewee, McDowell took a moment to survey the scene. The skies were blue, autumn in the Midwest was taking hold, Michael Jordan, one of the greatest sportsmen who ever lived, was a few feet away, chatting to Luke Donald.

Sergio García was still punching the air, celebrating Europe's first point of another great adventure, Furyk was looking more lugubrious than ever and less and less like Jimbo, and Snedeker was shaking his head in disbelief. The pressure of this compelling, endlessly dramatic competition had just reduced him to jelly.

McDowell drank it all in and turned to his girlfriend, Kristin, who was witnessing the competition for the first time. 'Welcome to the Ryder Cup,' McDowell said. 'Hope you enjoyed yourself.'

4   Just me and Tiger

The last game out on Friday morning was the one everyone wanted to see. Steve Stricker and Tiger Woods v Justin Rose and Ian Poulter. Stricker and Rose were fine players who would come to play defining roles in the outcome of this Ryder Cup but in this match they were cast in supporting roles. This was about Woods versus Poulter.

Woods does not like Poulter. That much is common knowledge. His antipathy towards him was recorded in excruciating detail in *The Big Miss*, the book released by Woods' former coach Hank Haney six months before the Ryder Cup. Haney had apparently intended *The Big Miss* to be a 'pure' golf book but it ended up reading like a kiss and tell.

It was full of fascinating insights into the golfer, including his repeated flirtations with the idea of turning his back on the sport to pursue a career in the military. In 2004, Haney wrote, Woods had gone to Fort Bragg, North Carolina, to do four days of Army special operations training. He made two tandem parachute jumps and took part in hand-to-hand combat exercises. Later, he became increasingly drawn to joining the US Navy's special operations sea, air and land teams, known as SEALs.

But the book felt cheap, too. It felt like a betrayal of confidence. There were passages that delved into Woods' marriage with his ex-wife, Elin, and which made her appear like a naïf. More and more, it read like Haney attempting to exact revenge on Woods because he had wanted Woods to be his friend and Woods saw him as a coach and nothing more.

So there are passages in the book that make Haney look pathetic. 'When we were watching television after dinner, he'd sometimes go to the refrigerator to get a sugar-free popsicle,' Haney wrote. 'But he never offered me one and one night I really wanted one of those popsicles. But I found myself sitting kind of frozen, not knowing what to do next . . .

'It actually took me a while to summon the courage to blurt out, "hey, bud, do you think I could have one of those popsicles?" He looked at me as if puzzled that I was asking and said "yeah, sure, go ahead and get one". I did but even after that, Tiger never offered me a popsicle.'

But *The Big Miss* also gave an insight into Woods' relationships with other players. Haney wrote that the players Woods liked tended to be quiet, modest, hard-working golfers like Jim Furyk and Steve Stricker. Woods respected men like Furyk and Stricker and admired their work ethic but he knew they did not have the talent to pose a consistently serious threat to him.

Furyk and Stricker were also the players he felt most comfortable playing with in the Ryder Cup. When Hal Sutton paired Woods with Phil Mickelson at Oakland Hills in 2004, it was a disaster. The body language between the two men veered between indifference, awkwardness and outright hostility. They lost both their games, first to Colin Montgomerie and Padraig Harrington, then to Darren Clarke and Lee Westwood.

Pairing Woods with Mickelson and expecting him to excel was a fundamental misjudgement of Woods' character.

Love knew that, which was why he stuck rigidly to playing him with Stricker. 'Tiger kept the supertalented at a distance,' Haney wrote. 'He didn't want players who could be a threat to feel comfortable around him. He was averse to loud and cocky players especially if he felt their records didn't warrant all the talk.'

For Woods, Poulter fitted into that category. He distrusted his brash attitude and his loud clothes. He talked big but he had never won a Major. Woods wanted to keep Poulter at arm's length but the two men both lived in Orlando and Haney recalled an incident in 2007 when Poulter asked for a lift back to Florida on Woods' private plane.

A couple of weeks before that year's US Open at Oakmont, near Pittsburgh, several players had arrived at the course on the same day to play a couple of practice rounds. When Poulter saw Woods, he had approached him and, knowing that Woods sometimes gave other Orlando-based players a lift to Florida on his plane, asked how they were getting home.

'But Tiger did that for guys he liked,' Haney wrote, 'and he didn't particularly like Poulter. Tiger gave a kind of non-committal answer and hoped Poulter would take the hint and find an alternative. But at the day's end, there was Poulter at the jetport, acting as if Tiger had said "yes". Tiger stretched out on his regular spot in the two seats in the front right of the plane and immediately put on his headphones.

'That left me to talk to Ian, which I didn't mind because I got along with him. As we were conversing, Tiger texted me. "Can you believe how this dick mooched a ride on my plane?" As far as I know, Ian didn't get any more rides.'

That incident only became general knowledge with the publication of Haney's book but there were other exchanges involving Poulter and Woods that had long been in the public

The Opening Ceremony of the 39th Ryder Cup at Medinah Country Club brought together two of the strongest teams ever assembled.

Europe captain José María Olazábal, far left, surveys the men who will attempt to retain the Ryder Cup.

MIKE EHRMANN/GETTY IMAGES

ROSS KINNAIRD/GETTY IMAGES

Olazábal's speech at the Opening Ceremony avoided any of the gaffes that had afflicted Sir Nick Faldo the last time Europe played in the States.

Olazábal chokes up during one of the many tributes to his late friend, the great Severiano Ballesteros.

Lee Westwood tees off at the first on Friday morning. Spectators had begun arriving long before dawn.

Tiger Woods endures another day of suffering at a Ryder Cup. Woods lost each of the three games in which he played on Friday and Saturday.

DAVID CANNON/GETTY IMAGES

ROSS KINNAIRD/GETTY IMAGES

Sergio Garcia and Rory McIlroy's caddie, JP Fitzgerald, share a more relaxed moment on the Friday morning.

Jim Furyk chips from the back of the green during the Friday morning foursomes. He and Brandt Snedeker lost narrowly to Rory McIlroy and Graeme McDowell.

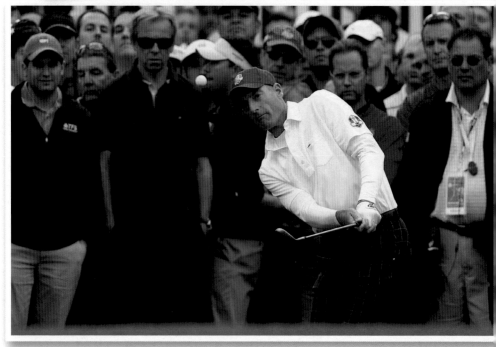

ROSS KINNAIRD/GETTY IMAGES.

Keegan Bradley, the dynamo of the US team, completes victory for him and Phil Mickelson on Friday morning.

DAVID CANNON/GETTY IMAGES

Mickelson and Bradley, who formed such a devastating partnership, celebrate victory over Luke Donald and Sergio García.

ROSS KINNAIRD/GETTY IMAGES.

Left: Justin Rose and Ian Poulter, Europe's most successful pairing at Medinah, line up a putt together during their Friday morning foursomes victory.

Right: Rose and Poulter celebrate after beating Tiger Woods and Steve Stricker 2&1. The triumph was sweet revenge for Poulter.

ANDY LYONS/GETTY IMAGES.

MIKE EHRMANN/GETTY IMAGES

Left: Bubba Watson and Webb Simpson confer over a putt during their Friday afternoon fourballs demolition of Peter Hanson and Paul Lawrie .

Main picture: Watson, the biggest hitter on the US team, crushes an approach shot to the 14th green.

Lawrie and Hanson try to work out a way to get back into the match.

DAVID CANNON.

MIKE EHRMANN/GETTY IMAGES.

Hanson congratulates Simpson on the 14th green after he and Lawrie fell to a humiliating 5&4 defeat to Simpson and Watson.

domain. Before the 2011 US Masters, Poulter caused a stir by saying he did not think Woods would finish in the top five at the tournament. His prediction was mentioned to Woods who responded with one of his best icy smiles. 'Poulter is always right, isn't he?' Woods said. He finished tied for fourth.

Perhaps most famously of all, Poulter gave an interview to *Golf World* magazine in March 2008 that made it clear he saw a future where he was Woods' only serious rival for the title of the sport's top player. Poulter was the world number 22 at the time and Woods was in his pre-fire hydrant pomp, away in the distance as the number one.

'The trouble is I don't rate anyone else,' Poulter said. 'Don't get me wrong, I respect everyone who is a professional. But the problem is I haven't played to my full potential yet. And when that happens it will just be me and Tiger.'

The interview caused hilarity and spawned the obvious comparisons. Woods had won 13 Majors at that point, Poulter none. Woods had won 85 tournaments, Poulter seven. But that was not really the point. Poulter was not attempting to diminish Woods. In fact, he paid him a handsome tribute. He was merely saying he believed there would be a time when he was a viable challenger to Woods' pre-eminence in the game.

There were reports at the time that Poulter's fellow professionals were planning a stunt where they would all depart the driving range at the same time, leaving just Woods and Poulter practising, but that never occurred. Instead, Woods wandered past Poulter in a locker room at a tournament a few weeks later and greeted him warmly. 'Hey, Number 2,' he said.

Woods didn't forget, either. He kept the gag going. After a dramatic win in Dubai later that year, against a field that included Poulter, Woods was asked about the gap between himself and the world's second-ranked player, Phil Mickelson. 'I thought Ian Poulter was Number 2,' he said.

So when Poulter went out on to the tee at 8.05 a.m. that first morning and heard the screaming and saw the American flags waving, all that was at the back of his mind. Sure, he was tense and coiled because this was his first taste of another Ryder Cup, the competition where he had established himself as a leader in the European team, a competition where he revels in the atmosphere.

But because he was playing Woods, it was about more than that. It was about answering the ridicule he had been subjected to when he said that one day he could be as good as Woods. It was about providing a riposte to the scorn Woods had reserved for him when he had asked for a lift on his plane. It was about proving to Woods and to everyone else that Woods had been wrong to disrespect him.

Poulter was coming off his best year ever at the Majors. He was seventh at the Masters, tied for ninth at The Open and tied for third at the PGA. But he had still found it hard to shake the impression that he was the sport's court jester, a man whose flamboyant dress sense and loud style camouflaged the fact that he had never won one of the biggest tournaments in the game.

It was easy to write him off as a clothes horse, a man who enjoyed the trappings of his success a little too much, who was a little too quick to post pictures on Twitter of his Bentley Continental GT, his Ferrari California and his Aston Martin DB9. Some had once dismissed him, as Paul Hayward wrote in the *Daily Telegraph*, as 'a clothes horse who was using golf as a vehicle to an empty kind of fame'.

Poulter had fed the image of the wide-boy Cockney with the fashion choices he made at high-profile tournaments. His trousers, in particular, have excited comment. There was the Union Jack pair Poulter wore at The Open at Royal Troon in 2004, that were described as 'the most garish attire in the event's 133-year history'.

Poulter was unapologetic. 'I'm always trying to be different,' he said. 'I don't like the way most people dress on the golf course. I think it's pretty bland, pretty boring. People were smiling and laughing and I received a few loud wolf whistles. It's good to go out there and enjoy it and let the spectators enjoy it as well.'

The next year, Poulter wore trousers emblazoned with a picture of the Claret Jug. 'That's the closest he'll ever get to it,' Seve Ballesteros said. In 2006 he was reprimanded for wearing an Arsenal shirt for a round at the Abu Dhabi championships. He wore a clinging gold lamé top at the Johnnie Walker Classic in India and the US Masters organizers had to warn him against turning up at the tournament with his hair dyed red as a tribute to his favourite football team.

What you wear says nothing about your talent with a golf club but his clothes sometimes made it easy for those who were looking for reasons to discredit Poulter to dismiss him as one big gimmick. Poulter was not keen on convention and in a sport that is draconian in its intolerance of disobedience, it made him an easy target.

He has spoken openly about how hatred of rejection and disgust for failure are two of the things that drive him on. But his career, from its earliest days, has also been about a struggle for acceptance. He did not follow a gilded path. He came from a working class family and paying to pursue a career in golf stretched their means. He was an assistant pro at Chesfield Downs Golf and Country Club near Stevenage, Hertfordshire, working in the club shop, selling tee pegs and Mars Bars.

Still, his outwardly brash attitude made it simple to write him off as a man for whom image was everything, a dilettante, a guy who valued style over substance, a chav in a world of snobbery. The *Guardian* called him 'an attention-seeking prat' after he had told everyone that it would be 'just me and Tiger'. But if his comments about becoming the only challenger to Woods' dominance were badly timed and a little over-ambitious, by the time he arrived at Medinah, no one could dispute Poulter's pedigree in the sport.

In addition to his 2012 record in the Majors (he was also one of only seven players to make the cut at all four Majors in 2007), he won the WGC-Accenture Match Play Championship in Arizona in 2010, which moved him to fifth in the world rankings. The following year he won the Volvo World Match Play Championship in Casares, Spain, beating Luke Donald in the final.

And most of all, there was the Ryder Cup. Poulter was the opposite of Woods in the competition. Where Woods seemed emasculated by the format, Poulter was empowered. He made his debut at Oakland Hills in 2004, playing just once on the first two days when he and Darren Clarke lost to Woods and Chris Riley in the Saturday morning fourballs.

But in 2008, chosen by Nick Faldo as one of his captain's picks, he was the star of the team. He won four points at Valhalla and was the outstanding performer in the European team that was defeated 16½ to 11½. Valhalla established Poulter as one of the European kingpins at the Ryder Cup, the bearer of the flame, the heir to Colin Montgomerie. Time and again, Poulter seemed to be able to raise his game for the competition and perform at a higher level than he could at the Majors. The format, the atmosphere, the pride of representing his country and his continent, all inspired him.

He arrived at Medinah with a Ryder Cup record of 8–3–0, although two of the three losses were in matches that involved Woods. When he appeared at the Media Centre for his pre-competition interview on the Wednesday before the action started, it was obvious he was relishing everything that the Ryder Cup would bring.

'It's absolutely magnificent to be wearing this jersey with a crest on it,' Poulter said, looking down at his team kit. 'It is always a very proud moment to be part of a great team. I'm one of those guys that are going to be out there enjoying the electricity. I think Chicago is a great sporting town, and this is going to be a very loud week. So I would expect them to be very vocal. I think everybody's ready for that. And I think for me, it adds to the electricity, adds to the adrenalin rush, and I can't wait to be part of the fun for three days.

'I don't really know why I've played so well in the competition in the past. I just love this event more than any other event in the world. I get very excited to play. I get very proud to put this shirt on and have that crest on my chest. I want to give it my all. I just love it. I was transfixed in '93 watching my first Ryder Cup, and things haven't changed since.'

Poulter was still working in a golf club shop in 1993 and he and two other assistants, Mike Isaacs and David Dennier, lived under canvas during the Ryder Cup. They found a house about three miles from the course and the woman who owned it let them pitch their tent in her back garden for £3 a night. They ate tinned food each night and drank wine from bottles.

'I wanted to play golf for a living but it was all a bit speculative,' Poulter said. 'But in 1993, I was there when Nick Faldo had his hole-in-one in his singles match against Paul Azinger. That Ryder Cup changed my opinion on golf. It gave me the drive to be the best player I could be. That's where I set myself the goals, so to come from being outside those ropes to playing my fourth Ryder Cup is more than a dream come true. But for that year at The Belfry, I might not have chased down any of my golf dreams.'

In the days leading up to Medinah, some suggested that the rivalry between the US and Europe would inevitably be dulled because so many of the European players, including Poulter, now lived in the golf enclave of Lake Nona, near Orlando. Poulter mocked that idea.

'We'll never lose that edge,' he said, 'because it's the Ryder Cup. It means too much to Europe. It means too much to us for it ever to lose that edge. This event is unique. I mean, you know, I hate to say we don't get on for three days, but there is that divide, and it's not that we don't like each other. We are all good friends, both sides of the pond. But there's something about Ryder Cup which kind of intrigues me how you can be great mates with somebody, but, boy, do you want to kill them in Ryder Cup. It's great. I mean, it's passion like I've never seen before. I love it. I love that chance to be able to go out there and beat one of your mates.'

Poulter's comments about wanting to kill his rivals in the Ryder Cup created a brief flurry of headlines but they did not have a lasting impact. Paul Casey had said a few years earlier that he 'properly hated' Americans in the aftermath of the Ryder Cup at Oakland Hills. Casey's point was that the partisan support at Oakland Hills, the repetitious 'USA, USA, USA' chants and Americans' sometimes insular nature made them easy to dislike for the duration of the competition. He found it hard to shake off the comments but Poulter moved on seamlessly.

His belligerent attitude during Ryder Cups, though, did make him a marked man. His intensity, his confrontational stance, his inability to disguise just how desperate he was to beat his opponent, his clenched-fist celebrations that accompanied every holed putt, his repeated high-fives with his partner that accompanied every crucial moment, made him the player most Americans loved to hate and hated to lose to.

'I like to compete and I like to win – doesn't matter who it is,' Stricker said in the build-up to Medinah, 'but when it comes down to playing Ian Poulter in the Ryder Cup, I don't want to lose to him.' Stricker had lost twice to Poulter at Valhalla and had become particularly vexed, he said, by the way Poulter's eyes bulged every time he holed an important putt. 'When he yells and screams, they bug out,' Stricker said. 'That's why you want to beat him. He's a big-time competitor. You can tell he's working hard at it and wanting to beat you. And when you come across a guy who really wants to beat you, you really want to beat him.'

Other resentments lingered with the Americans where Poulter was concerned, too. At Celtic Manor in 2010, just before the singles began, he was interviewed live on television about his forthcoming match with Matt Kuchar. Poulter told the interviewer: 'I will deliver my point.' Woods was watching in the US team room and, incensed, hurried to the locker room to tell Kuchar what Poulter had said.

The Americans usually love a sporting guarantee – New York Jets quarterback Joe Namath pioneered the genre by guaranteeing that his team would beat the Baltimore Colts in the 1969 Super Bowl – but they did not take so kindly to the one that Poulter made.

Poulter spoke about it to the *Daily Telegraph*'s golf correspondent Jamie Corrigan a couple of days before Medinah. In the course of his piece, Corrigan floated the idea that a lot of the things Poulter does are intended to heap pressure on himself, to make him even more afraid to fail. Corrigan included the way Poulter dresses as part of the theory.

The idea was that if you dressed in Union Flag trousers, you had better play well or you are going to look twice as stupid as everyone else. No chance of sloping away from the course unnoticed after a bad round if you have got a giant image of the Claret Jug emblazoned on your left trouser leg, either.

'Some people were offended by the guarantee at Celtic Manor, sure,' Poulter said. 'But in my mind, Tiger went in there and tried to fire his guy up. That's what the Ryder Cup is all about – passion. And whatever you feel you have to do to whip up the fire, you just have to do it. I didn't mean to be disrespectful although I suppose it's hard not to sound disrespectful when you say you're definitely going to beat someone. But I said it for a reason. I'm not sure I could have wanted to win any more, but by saying that, it put even more pressure on me to win. I would have been slated if I hadn't won after that comment. I also wanted to show my team how confident I was. I felt very good at the time. It came off. It was fine.'

It certainly came off. Poulter made good on his promise at Celtic Manor. He outclassed Kuchar 5&4, the biggest individual European victory in that Ryder Cup. From then on, his European teammates began calling him 'The Postman' because he always delivered. It was an old line – the NBA's Utah Jazz forward Karl Malone was known as The Mailman back in the 1980s and 1990s for the same reason – but Poulter loved it.

'Nothing comes close to getting me up for it like the Ryder Cup,' Poulter said, 'not even remotely. You only get three days at it and it goes very quickly. So every one you play in you kind of cherish more and more.' He said that maybe he had an affinity with the competition because he was a frustrated footballer. 'In football, you show more emotion in ten minutes than you do in the whole week of a normal golf tournament,' he said. 'So yeah, maybe that does have something to do with my Ryder Cup fascination. It's the one place a golfer can totally interact with fans.'

His attitude to the competition enthused his teammates, too. They laughed when he went into his wild celebrations but only because they seemed slightly unnerved by his intensity and awed by the way he used the energy from the crowds and from the thrill of representing a team to take his player to a higher level.

'He and I won a fourball at Valhalla when he birdied the eighteenth,' Graeme McDowell recalled. 'I woke up the next morning and my arm was sore. I couldn't work out why and then I remembered. We were high-fiving each other so hard because he gets so charged up. No one can strut around like Poults. It's great. He's the guy I'd love to play with again.'

There was one guy Poulter wanted to play with, too. Or rather play against. It was Woods. It was not necessarily because a perceived enmity had grown up between them, although Poulter must have been hurt by Woods' scathing appraisal of him in *The Big Miss*. Whatever effect that had on Poulter, he kept it to himself. He refused to rise to questions that alluded to Woods referring to him as a 'dick' and he would not discuss the fall-out from his 'mooching' a lift on Woods' plane.

But despite his own excellence in the Ryder Cup and Woods' struggles, Poulter had never beaten him in the competition and he wanted a chance to put that right. His first taste of the Ryder Cup had been that defeat to Woods and Riley at Oakland Hills and he and Ross Fisher had lost to Woods and Stricker at Celtic Manor. Poulter's only other Ryder Cup defeat came at Valhalla when he and Rose lost to Stewart Cink and Chad Campbell in the Friday morning foursomes.

'Of the three games I've lost in eleven Ryder Cup matches, Tiger's been responsible for two of them,' Poulter said. 'For that reason, and that reason only, I'd like another crack at him.'

Now, as he stood on the first tee at Medinah early on Friday morning, he was about to get his chance.

5 Done mooching

It happens every time. Every time Tiger Woods stands on the first tee at the beginning of a Ryder Cup, everyone thinks this will be the one. This will be the one where he performs like one of the greatest players of all time, this will be the one where his play is not a crushing disappointment, this will be the one where he wins it for America instead of chucking it away.

This will be the one where he proves he can be a great team player as well. It is not that he has never played well at Ryder Cups. In fact, he has a more than respectable singles record. It is just that his indomitability in individual events has never quite translated into team play when it comes to representing the USA against Europe.

It is hard to reconcile the Woods who has won 14 Majors and who has been regarded with awe by most of his competitors with the Woods who has one of the lousiest records in Ryder Cup history. It is hard to look at the man who has so often seemed disengaged at Ryder Cups with the player who has brought an unparalleled intensity to competing in Majors.

The theories explaining the discrepancies between Major Tiger and Ryder Tiger are many and varied. The most common one is that Woods simply does not do 'team'. He is a solitary man who has made a point of being separate throughout his career and has used his isolation to intimidate rivals or at the very least unsettle them.

He does not want anybody to get close. He does not want to have any buddies. Not among the best players in the States anyway. He does not want them to feel comfortable with him. And maybe he does not want to feel comfortable with them. He wants to retain the competitive edge. He wants to make sure the sharp edges of his ruthlessness are not blunted in any way.

So the Ryder Cup makes him uneasy. It is a forced kind of bonding that just does not work for him. And he does not really try. He has never sought to forge a bond with one of the rising stars of the game as Phil Mickelson did with Keegan Bradley at Medinah, for instance. He is not interested in passing on tips or helping guys out. Since 2004, he has played only with Steve Stricker or Jim Furyk and that's it. Period.

Part of it, perhaps, is that his aura is diminished when he plays with a partner. His greatness is diluted. His ability to intimidate an opponent is halved. Perhaps some of that aura has gone anyway now after the car crash outside his home in November 2009 unleashed a wave of revelations about his personal life and a break from the sport.

Woods has gradually fought his way back to the top of the game since then and is a contender again. But it is not the same as it used to be. He is not quite the ruthless closer he once was and others, notably Rory McIlroy, have stepped up to challenge him. Woods still has the history but it is McIlroy that most now regard as the best player in the world.

'I think it's very difficult to be critical of Tiger in the Ryder Cup,' Graeme McDowell said during one of his Medinah interviews. 'It's a huge game for an underdog to play a Tiger

Woods, and they get up for it. They are not expected to win. When expectation levels drop, a player's game tends to improve. A guy who plays Tiger Woods, or a player of that calibre, doesn't expect to win so he lets it all go and he plays out of his skin and gets the upset.'

It is still unthinkable not to have Woods in the US team when he is available, but it should not be. The only time he has missed a Ryder Cup was in 2008 when he underwent knee surgery. The US seemed to do just fine without him at Valhalla. They won for the first time since 1999. That meant that going into Medinah, Woods had played on six Ryder Cup teams and won just once.

For Woods, golf is the Majors. That is how he measures his career. That is how he wants to be remembered. That is where he knows his greatness lies. The Ryder Cup is something off to the side, something you don't even get paid for. In 2002, in the build-up to that year's Ryder Cup at The Belfry, he was about to play for the $1m first prize at the World Golf Championship Match Play tournament at Mount Juliet in Ireland when he was asked whether he would rather win the tournament or the Ryder Cup the following week.

'This week,' Woods said.

'Why?' he was asked.

'I can think of a million reasons,' he said.

Woods' target from the very start has been to better Jack Nicklaus's record of 18 Major victories. 'Anyone in golf could tell you how many Majors Jack won, but who knows his Ryder Cup record?' Woods asked a few years ago.

Maybe there has been an element of scorn involved, too. Golf, like tennis, is about mental toughness as well as skill. There is an inner game to be played and you win a Major on your own with no one else to rely on, playing against the course and those around you. In the Ryder Cup, not only do you have to rely on others but others rely on you. You could be mentally weak and still succeed in the Ryder Cup, and Woods abhorred that.

The foursomes, in particular, when teammates alternately play one ball, has always disconcerted him. His game is about order and putting the ball in the right place. In foursomes he is confronted with a situation where he has to try to clear up someone else's mess. Either that or watch someone else ruin his perfect approach play. Except that such has been Woods' distaste for the format that often he has been the weaker player in a pair.

His body language at Ryder Cups has often been shocking. At Oakland Hills in 2004, he seemed appalled to have been paired with Mickelson. At one hole, rather than wait on the tee while Mickelson drove off in a foursomes match, Woods took a short cut and went to wait halfway down the fairway.

Technically, there was nothing wrong with what he did but it went against the spirit of the competition. The camaraderie between him and Mickelson was zero.

There was one priceless moment at Oakland Hills when Mickelson hit a terrible tee-shot at the 18th. This time, Woods was standing next to him but when the camera shifted on to him, he had a look of disgust on his face.

'He was trying to do it all by himself when he first broke into the team,' Davis Love admitted before Medinah. 'He was the dominant player in the game and he was trying to give performances that reflected that. When you're that good it takes time to learn that you have to be part of the team rather than be the team, that you have to win points with the help of your partners. It is what Michael Jordan had to learn, that if someone gives you the ball, you give the ball back.

I think Tiger has learned. That's the Tiger we will see at this Ryder Cup.'

The suspicion was that Love was whistling to keep his spirits up. America had been looking for Woods for leadership for more than a decade and had never got it. Why should Medinah be any different? 'Europe Beware: Whisper it But Woods Looks Like a Team Player at Last' a headline in the *Daily Mail* read during the build-up. Really? There was no evidence for that. It was just more of the same reliance on the law of averages, the belief that sooner or later the real Tiger had to show up at the Ryder Cup.

Woods accepted that he had not lived up to expectations in Ryder Cup play. In fact, in the week leading up to Medinah, he was happy to take the blame for Europe's domination of the event in the 21st century, a period of mastery that coincided neatly with his own hegemony in the Majors.

'Well, certainly I am responsible for that,' Woods said, 'because I didn't earn the points that I was put out there for. I believe I was out there, what, in five sessions each time, and I didn't go 5–0 on our side. So I certainly am a part of that, and that's part of being a team. I needed to go get my points for my team, and I didn't do that. Hopefully I can do that this week, and hopefully the other guys can do the same and we can get this thing rolling.'

Woods was the antithesis of Poulter. Where Poulter grew in team competition, Woods shrank. Where Poulter thrived on the idea of winning for his team, Woods faded away. Where Poulter played better when he had a teammate by his side, Woods played worse. The disparity between the golf Woods played at the Ryder Cup and the golf he played at the Majors was one of the great conundrums of modern sport.

Woods knew going into Medinah that if he could not

improve his Ryder Cup numbers, it would be a stain on his career. Best at something, worst at something else, people would say when it was over. The Majors might be his measuring stick but others would look at his failure to perform for his country and condemn him for it. A Ryder Cup record of 13 wins, 14 losses and two matches halved had very little to commend it when you had a claim to be the best golfer who ever lived.

Davis Love sought to make more excuses for him. US captains always do. There is no point criticizing Woods because at the Ryder Cup, except in 2010 when Corey Pavin made him a captain's pick, they're stuck with him. So they have to do their best to talk about him with reverence as if he's the Woods that excels in stroke-play events and pretend they know nothing about his previous outings as an Average Joe in the Ryder Cup.

'Match play is just so different,' Love said. 'Tiger can play great and his partner not play well, or the other team can play extremely well. There's probably a lot of times where it's just a matter of who you're up against. The other thing is that somebody has to play in Tiger's bubble. You have to be a special guy to be able to handle that.'

The problem is that at the Ryder Cup, Tiger doesn't appear to be able to handle Tiger's bubble either. He had won two of his 14 Majors at Medinah, the US PGA championships in 1999 and 2006, but after he had exchanged an icy handshake with Poulter on the first tee, Woods promptly hooked his drive wildly to the left. So much for him having to clean up other people's mess. Stricker must have watched that drive fly and thought, 'Thanks, buddy.'

In 2006 at the K Club Woods had pulled his opening tee-shot into a lake and his first drive here was not much better. It was an improvement only because the Americans got lucky, received a free drop against a temporary fence and somehow saved par.

But Woods did not get any better. It turned into one of the worst rounds even he has played in the Ryder Cup. It was hapless, Keystone Cops stuff. Stricker found the lake off the tee at the par-three 2nd and Woods sliced his drive at the 5th, followed by a ricochet off a portable toilet. The way Woods was playing, sooner or later there were going to be casualties and at the 7th he felled a spectator with another wild drive that thudded into the man's head.

A marshall was holding an ice-pack to the man's head by the time Woods arrived to check if his victim was okay. As he sat dazed on the ground, Woods signed a glove for him. It was not enough to stop the bleeding, though. After Stricker missed the green at the par-three 8th, Woods' flop shot from the rough failed to reach the green. 'It was car-crash golf,' Neil McLeman, the *Daily Mirror*'s respected golf correspondent, wrote.

Poulter had put the Europeans 2 up on the 11th when he holed a shot out of the bunker, prompting a delighted fist-pumping reaction from Rose. Europe went 3 up at the 12th and even though the Americans pulled a shot back on the next, Poulter made birdie on the 14th to restore the three-shot advantage after Woods had managed to find a rare example of deep rough on this course. On the 15th Woods made yet another excursion into the trees only to see his ball bounce back on to the fairway off a branch, and Stricker secured a fortunate birdie. Europe 2 up.

Woods gave the Americans a glimpse of a half when he hit a beautiful long iron to the 16th green, but Stricker missed the long birdie putt and Poulter sank a nerveless 12-foot putt for par which halved the hole and made Europe dormie two. That prompted his biggest celebration of the round so far. There were others, needless to say, that would surpass it in the days that followed.

'That's me being me, I guess,' Poulter said of his antics at the 16th. 'Ryder Cup is like no other; you can't do that in any other situation. That really is how much it means. I've seen it over the years with Seve and Ollie and Faldo and all the guys. You know what, that's why Ryder Cup is so special, because you can hole that putt at the right time and it does mean that much, so your emotions just come out.'

Poulter denied suggestions that Olazábal had asked him to mute his celebrations in the interests of maintaining harmony between the two teams. 'Are you kidding me? Are you for real?' Poulter said. 'Are you going to tell someone not to enjoy holing a putt in front of 20,000 people and seeing them go bananas? That is Ryder Cup. That is what it means. Hell no.

'It's like scoring a penalty in a Champions League final. You should enjoy it. You haven't got the potential to hole many of them during the day so why not give it a fist pump? No, we haven't been told to tone down any enjoyment factor when trying to beat the opposition.

'At the sixteenth, I had hit a poor second shot, Tiger hit a great second shot and gave Stricker a chance to win that hole to get it to one down with two to play, which would have been key for them to try and do that. He misses that hole. I mean, those are the wonders of match play. Whether sometimes it's to halve the hole or to win the hole, putts of that length just mean so much.'

When the 17th was halved, too, the match was over. Europe had won 2&1 and Poulter finally had his first Ryder Cup victory over Woods. Woods had played so badly that there was immediate speculation that he would be dropped for the afternoon session, the first time a captain would have dared to do it in his Ryder Cup career. 'Never mind taking him off the course after eighteen holes,' Colin Montgomerie said on Sky, 'I'd have had him out of there after nine today.'

Most analysts nominated Woods' performance as the worst of all 16 players in the morning session. It felt all too predictable. It also gave Woods an unwanted record. The defeat to Poulter and Rose meant Woods had officially drawn level with Raymond Floyd as statistically the worst foursomes player in American Ryder Cup history. In 13 appearances in the format, he had now lost eight.

Poulter was delighted he had finally beaten Woods, delighted that the European victory had brought the scores all level at 2–2 after the first session. 'This for me was a tough game,' Poulter said. 'Tiger has had two of my three defeats and I never wanted to have another one. But as Justin said, I've got his back and he's got mine. He asks me to hole a putt, I'm going to go and deliver.'

When the afternoon pairings were announced, there was widespread surprise. Poulter had been rested but not Woods. Poulter was asked if he was shocked that Woods had not been left out after the way he had hacked his way around the course in the morning.

'Yeah, but he's Tiger Woods,' Poulter said. 'Is Davis Love going to sit Tiger Woods? He's a brave man if he does that. You know, he's Tiger Woods. He's the guy they get out there fired up. He didn't quite fire them up this morning but you never know. When Tiger is on, he's on and he's very impressive but when he's not, he's not. Still, it's a brave captain to leave him out.'

Poulter was asked if it would be equally difficult for Olazábal to leave out McIlroy if the circumstances seemed to demand it. Poulter said that Woods' status in the game, the fact that he had been acknowledged as the greatest player in the world for so long, that his pre-eminence had been unchallenged, made him a different case.

'I think it's completely different,' Poulter said. 'Tiger is Tiger, and Tiger is going to want to go out and play five matches. I mean, he knows if it clicks, at any moment out there on the first few holes, if he finds his form, then he's going to be a very tough man to beat.'

He denied he was disappointed that he had been left out for the afternoon fourballs. 'I would love to have played five matches,' Poulter said, 'but I realize that we are a team. That team is very, very, very strong this year, and Ollie really wanted to kind of get everybody playing on Friday. So four guys have got to change from the morning round, and that's obviously going to be difficult. He said to me that he would like to keep me fresh going through Saturday, Sunday.'

So Poulter bit his tongue. He had already won his first point and achieved another of his great ambitions by beating Woods at the Ryder Cup. As the match began to turn against Europe that afternoon, perhaps he sensed his team would soon be relying on him more than ever.

6

America's new hero and his collection of idiosyncrasies

By the time Ian Poulter's foursomes showdown with Tiger Woods had reached its conclusion, a worrying new dimension to the competition had emerged for Europe. Poulter brought great energy to his team, the kind of energy that the US had always struggled to match. By Friday lunchtime, it was clear that that struggle was over.

Too often, the US side has looked like a pale imitation of the European team at the Ryder Cup. Too often, they have seemed like a collection of individuals who have felt profoundly awkward in each other's company. In the years of its recent hegemony, Europe has established a monopoly on camaraderie and team bonding that has led to prolonged bouts of soul-searching in the States.

But that shifted at Medinah. That was one of the reasons why it turned into such an epic competition. New blood flooded the American team and refreshed it and rejuvenated it. There were many times in the opening two days when the Europeans were the ones who looked tired and old and jaded. The US reclaimed their youth and rediscovered their passion for the concept of the team. Suddenly, it was the American players who looked like they were having the time of their lives.

The epitome of the pumped-up solidarity that had infused the US team was a precociously talented 26-year-old from Vermont called Keegan Bradley. Bradley was already a star. He had won the first Major he ever played in, the 2011 PGA Championship in Atlanta, and now, a year later, he was becoming the emotional driving force of a reborn US team.

Bradley was full of idiosyncrasies. He took an age to play every shot, walking up to the ball once then retreating from it. He looked a bit like a dog worrying a stick. And when he was judging a putt, he had a peculiar way of cocking his head to one side and fixing the ball with a one-eyed stare. 'Like a psychopath planning a dastardly deed,' one commentator noted. Wired and intense, it all added to his charisma.

Then, there was his spitting. It, too, seemed to be part of a hyperactive personality. He spat hundreds of times during a televised tournament at the Riviera Club outside Los Angeles a few months before the Ryder Cup and was heavily criticized for it. When Bradley watched the footage himself, he was horrified.

'I was very surprised to see the replay of the telecast to see how much I was spitting,' he said. 'To be honest with you, I really had no idea I was doing it. And I feel bad. I just ask everybody to just kind of bear with me as I go through this, because it's something I've done without even knowing it. But I will do my best to stop.

'It's something that I'm glad has come up, because I'm able to kind of nip it now. The players have all been so nice, and I did get a ton of good responses when I apologized. And I'm so thankful I'm playing this week, so I can confront this. Hopefully,

I can play well, get my face back on camera and show that I'm dealing with it.'

By the time he got to Medinah, the spitting was no longer an issue. Instead, Bradley brought incredible enthusiasm with him to the Ryder Cup. He said that walking to the first tee for his first practice round on Tuesday was the proudest moment of his career. This was from a man who had won a Major championship.

Bradley was steeped in the history of the tournament and of team golf. His aunt, Pat Bradley, was a famous US woman golfer and member of Solheim Cup teams. Bradley remembered watching her and being shown her golf bag with the Stars and Stripes stitched into it.

And if one of the seminal moments in Poulter's life was watching Nick Faldo and Paul Azinger at The Belfry in 1993, Bradley remembered being hoisted on his father's shoulders as a 13-year-old and watching the incredible scenes of the American comeback at Brookline in 1999 unfolding before his eyes.

Bradley bought into the spirit of the Ryder Cup right from the start. It helped that Davis Love had paired him with Phil Mickelson for the Friday morning foursomes match against Luke Donald and Sergio García, who had played together four times in the format and never been beaten. Neither of the Europeans, in fact, had ever lost a foursomes match, whoever they had been paired with.

Bradley had grown up idolizing Mickelson and was not shy about talking about it. In turn, Mickelson had taken it upon himself to act as a mentor for Bradley and had organized a series of practice rounds with the younger man in the build-up to Medinah, rounds which Bradley said he wanted to impress in so badly that they were the perfect preparation for the pressure of the Ryder Cup.

Bradley arrived at Medinah before any of the players from either team on Friday morning. He was on the range a couple of hours before dawn, practising by floodlight. He might have been one of the four rookies on the US team but it was already clear he planned to hit his stride early and take a leading role.

Donald was there early, too. He had made his home in Chicago and met his wife, Diane, there and was hoping that he would attract some local support as a result. He had even mapped out his ideal itinerary if he had a day to show his teammates around the city.

'I would probably start off at Wrigley Field,' Donald said, talking about the atmospheric old stadium that is the home of the Chicago Cubs baseball team. 'We'd have a few beers in Lincoln Park and then catch a Cubs game. Then maybe go down to Michigan Avenue to check out some of the sights down there. Buckingham Fountain. The Bean. Just take in the city, really. I've travelled around most of America and I always get drawn back to Chicago. I just love the culture.'

But when the players assembled on the first tee, the cheers were all for Bradley and Mickelson. Bradley loved it. He worked the crowd like a veteran, whirling his arms in the air, exhorting them to make more noise. 'Major winner, Major winner,' they sang back at him in response, a brutal reminder to Donald and García of their failure to win any of the game's biggest individual honours.

The Americans started well and went 1 up at the second with a birdie and although Donald and García levelled the scores and briefly led, Bradley made an eight-foot putt for a birdie at the 9th hole that turned the momentum in favour of the Americans. Bradley stirred up the crowd again after that putt, feeding on their fervour.

It was already clear from their chemistry and the way they were encouraging each other that Bradley and Mickelson, another of America's golfing greats with a mediocre Ryder Cup record, were a partnership made in heaven. All square after 11 holes, Bradley and Mickelson suddenly accelerated away from the Europeans, winning four holes in succession.

Bradley was superb on the back nine and it was he who sealed the victory when he buried a 30-foot putt on the 15th to put the match out of the reach of Donald and García and hand them their first defeat in foursomes. It was a victory that the Americans felt carried great symbolism, a downing of Europe's strongest pair led by one of their own rookies.

Because the match finished before the game between McIlroy and McDowell and Furyk and Snedeker, it was also the first point on the board. The omens were good for the States and when Bradley and Mickelson walked the final holes with Furyk and Snedeker, lending their support, they were greeted with uproarious cheers by the American fans, hailed as the standard-bearers for the attempt to win back the Cup.

Love announced that he would be sending them back out together in the afternoon and they were drawn against McIlroy and McDowell. First, though, they grabbed a bit of lunch and enthused about each other's play, much to the amusement of Bradley's girlfriend, Jillian Stacey, and Mickelson's wife, Amy.

'They're infatuated with each other,' she said afterwards. 'They couldn't stop talking about each other. It was like, "Oh that shot you hit was so great." "No, that putt of yours was even better." "But I couldn't have done it without your amazing read." Every now and then they would stare into each other's eyes like they were a long-lost love. At some point Amy was like, "It's a good thing we're here, or they might start talking about getting married."'

By the end of lunch, Mickelson and Bradley knew that the morning foursomes had ended all square. Poulter and Rose had closed out their game and Zach Johnson and Jason Dufner had eased past Lee Westwood and Francesco Molinari 3&2. Westwood and Molinari was a pairing that had not worked. Westwood, so often one of the most inspirational European players, had seemed curiously muted.

Mickelson and Bradley went out second in the afternoon fourballs and promptly won the first three holes against McIlroy and McDowell. That made seven holes in succession. Somehow, the Americans managed to maintain the same emotional pitch in the afternoon as they had set in the morning. McIlroy and McDowell struggled to get back into the game.

The Americans saw it as a pivotal clash. Love had already sensed that Mickelson and Bradley would be a crucial pairing and he and Woods had talked candidly about the importance of going after McIlroy and puncturing the aura around him. He was the world number one but they wanted to show that meant nothing to them. They believed that if they could beat him, it would dent the air of confidence that the Europeans had preserved from past triumphs.

They wanted to put pressure on McIlroy, not just to damage the level of his performance but to set an example to the rest of the American team. Bradley and Mickelson did the job to perfection. Bradley, doing his best screen-villain impersonation, as he lined up his putts, was deadly in the early holes and sank five birdies as the Americans built that three-hole lead.

His play had another benefit to the Americans. It inspired Mickelson. Mickelson, who played in his first Ryder Cup in 1995 – when Bradley was a nine-year-old – had an even worse record than Woods in the competition. He might have won four Majors but going into Medinah, he had won just 14 points

from 34 matches. He had more losses than any American in Ryder Cup history and a reputation for going missing when his team needed him most.

But playing alongside Bradley, he looked like a different man. He seemed to revel in the competition and the drama. Energized by Bradley's wide-eyed, fast-twitch fervour, Mickelson got as high on adrenalin as his partner. Every time he strode off the green through the midst of the cheering, whooping galleries, Mickelson slapped hands with as many fans as he could, a huge grin plastered across his face. 'I don't think I've ever seen Phil this excited on a golf course,' his mother, Mary, said during Friday's play.

So when Bradley's level dropped a little on the back nine, Mickelson stepped up. He made a series of halves against McIlroy to keep the Europeans at bay at two strokes behind. On the 17th, a beautiful hole over water, Bradley landed his tee shot in a greenside bunker. With McIlroy and McDowell threatening to force their way back into the game, Mickelson hit his tee-shot to within a few feet of the flag.

'It was the best shot I've ever seen in my entire life,' Bradley said. 'Afterwards, we were running down the fairway, we had our arms around each other, we were screaming; it was like a Patriots game out there.' Or, borrowing from Amy Mickelson, a slow-mo sequence from *Love Story*.

Mickelson was just as high on the excitement of the occasion. Gone was the measured language of the pre-competition press conferences, his studied politeness and easy charm. In its place came words that spoke of a golfer in rapture. 'That baby was all over the flagstick,' he said about his tee-shot at the 17.

Mickelson sealed victory with a birdie at that hole and it was clear that the balance of power in the competition was swinging towards the Americans. The Europeans were startled.

Mickelson, so often a lamb in the Ryder Cup, had started to roar like a lion. It was the first time in nine editions of the competition that he had won two matches in the same day. A dramatic transformation appeared to be taking place in him.

'The way Keegan drives the golf ball off the tee,' Mickelson said, 'it just wears down your opponent, watching him hit the ball so long and straight. And the way he putts, it is just off the charts. It's been a real pleasure playing alongside him.'

With the two other veterans, Woods and Furyk, both struggling to post points, it was beginning to look like Mickelson and Bradley were the dream pair, rookie and veteran, east coast and west coast, wired and laid back. They were cutting a swathe through the Europeans and winding themselves up for more.

'This is one of the most emotional days playing a Ryder Cup that we'll ever have,' Mickelson, 42, said. 'This has been one of the biggest highs that we've had. I felt young, and it felt great. I had energy all day. I just felt terrific. I'd say to him, "Hey, I need a little pep talk," and he'd just give me something that would get me boosted right up, and I'd end up hitting a good shot.

'Keegan played some of the best golf and to be his partner was an awesome experience. I love, love playing with this man. He's just so fun, loves the game and plays with such excitement and man, can he roll the rock.'

It felt to Mickelson in those moments on Friday afternoon as though years of under-achievement and ridicule for the way he had played in Ryder Cups were being sluiced away. His popularity has grown and grown in recent years as the Majors have started to arrive and as Woods has endured such a spectacular fall from grace. Woods still enjoys the respect of most golf fans for everything he has achieved but Mickelson has their affection. As he and Bradley strode around Medinah, they were cheered with such abandon, they might have been the kings of America.

The fans were filled with a hope that they were witnessing the start of a new era, that Bradley was a symbol of a new generation that was about to rejuvenate American golf and provide a legitimate rival to Europe's wunderkind, McIlroy. In Bradley, they had a hero who seemed comfortable with their adulation, who seemed to grow and grow with every cheer.

The partners of Bradley and Mickelson kept their own rapport going, too. As they walked down one fairway, Jillian Stacey stopped and sounded a note of alarm.

'Oh, I'm sorry, Phil's in the trees,' Bradley's girlfriend said.

Amy Mickelson didn't miss a beat.

'He's used to it,' she said. 'He'll be fine.'

Afterwards, everyone wanted to talk about Bradley. He was anointed the man of the day. He was the one who had seized the moment. He was the one who had changed the momentum of the competition. He was the one who had seemed to signify a new beginning for American golf.

'Keegan's a great player and he's been playing well,' Love said. 'And he's got that intense look in his eye that the great players have. I was asking Phil, you know, "How are you going to handle Keegan? Are you going to help him with his putts or not help him?"

'Phil said, "As long as he gives them that little sideways look, you've got to let him do what he wants to do." My son and I were sitting on the side of one green, and Keegan turned his head like that and I said, "You know he's going to make this one," and right in it went. He's a competitor and he's confident in his game and he loves to be there. He loves walking out on that first tee.'

Bradley was keen not to be outdone in the orgy of mutual appreciation with his playing partner. It was beginning to feel as if he and Mickelson really ought to sit down in the team room and compose sonnets to each other.

'I felt so freed up because I knew wherever I hit it, Phil could hit an amazing shot to save the hole for us,' Bradley said. 'So I just freewheeled, which isn't necessarily easy to do in that format. It was one of the most memorable days of my life so far. I just loved every second of it. And being able to walk down the fairway with Phil and do this is a dream come true. It's another moment in my life that I can't believe I'm a part of. This is literally what I've dreamt about since I was a little kid. I got to do it next to my idol all day.'

Quite how Bradley got to sleep that night is anyone's guess. England's footballers, we have learned recently, routinely take sleeping pills to lull them into unconsciousness after matches because they have so much adrenalin zooming around their bodies. The way Bradley was wired up, it might have taken a tranquilizer dart to put him out.

At the end of his Friday afternoon press conference, he was asked whether, after 36 holes of high-octane golf on his emotionally supercharged Ryder Cup debut, he had any energy left.

'Oh, baby,' Bradley said. 'I wish I could go thirty-six more.'

7

Bubba Golf

Keegan Bradley's irrepressible, messianic enthusiasm was one thing but even at the Ryder Cup, no one had even seen anything quite like Bubba Watson's entrance that Friday afternoon. Watson, the flamboyant, happy-go-lucky, bible-thumping maverick of the US team, had been left out of the morning foursomes but when he and US Open champion Webb Simpson went out first in the fourballs against Paul Lawrie and Peter Hanson, Watson made up for lost time.

The crowd went wild as he and Simpson walked over the footbridge from the clubhouse and strode on to the first tee. Watson milked the applause as best he could but when he stepped up to press his tee peg into the turf and stood back to address his ball, the crowd, rowdy as they were, obeyed convention and fell silent.

Watson looked up disapprovingly. He moved his hands up and down by his side. The crowd could not quite believe it but his gestures were unambiguous. He wanted them to cheer while he was hitting his shot. In a sport where an inappropriately timed click of a camera shutter is met with a hard stare or a furious rebuke and anything but cathedral quiet is frowned upon as a player prepares to play, this was unheard of.

In the commentary box, Nick Faldo said that Old Tom Morris, the pioneer of professional golf and winner of The Open four times in the 1860s, would be spinning in his grave. Maybe, but no scene encapsulated Sky's promotional slogan 'It's golf but not as we know it' better than Watson unleashing his pink driver and lashing the ball down the fairway as thousands of fans roared with delight.

'I did it in Phoenix,' Watson said later, 'the regular tournament in Phoenix. So I've done it before with an iron. So I did it yesterday in the practice round just for the fun of it and then today. I figured if I was going to play bad today I'd better have fun on the first hole at least. So I just got the crowd into it. Just did it for fun. And then somehow I played good after that. But you know, I just did it for the fun of it. It's the Ryder Cup. Why not have fun? We made it here, and you got to enjoy your time here and have fun playing golf.'

Watson was far more than a crowd pleaser, of course. He had won the US Masters the previous April, hitting a miraculous shot out of the trees on the second hole of a play-off to beat South Africa's Louis Oosthuizen and win his first Major. Then he had promptly broken down in tears, sobbing uncontrollably in the arms of his mother, Molly, before slipping on his Green Jacket.

Watson, who was born on Guy Fawkes Night, was a singular character, an evangelistic, proselytizing Christian who had never had a golf lesson in his life and was the biggest hitter on the PGA Tour. He was an advocate of what he called 'Bubba Golf', a high-risk, high-reward approach to the game some way wide of orthodoxy.

'If I've got a swing, I've got a shot,' Watson explained. 'I just play golf, fun-loving Bubba, just try to have fun and goof around. I'm used to the woods. I'm used to the rough. In the play-off, I saw it was a perfect draw, a perfect hook.' When he won the Masters, Neil McLeman said in the *Daily Mirror* that he had the potential to be the new John Daly – 'without the divorces, the gambling and the alcoholism'.

Because if Watson has a similar approach to Daly or Phil Mickelson on the course, his life away from golf is very different to the Wild Thing's. 'Most important things in my life,' he wrote on Twitter after he had won the Masters. '1. God 2. Wife 3. Family 4. Helping others 5. Golf.'

He and his wife, Angie, who told him on their first date that she would never be able to have children, went through four years of heartache and struggle trying to adopt a baby until finally, just before his Masters victory, they were finally presented with a baby boy they called Caleb. Watson wondered aloud whether winning at Augusta might gain him a couple of weeks grace before he started changing nappies.

Watson is a regular at the PGA Tour's weekly Bible Study, held every Wednesday night during tournament weeks and attended by fellow professionals like Simpson, Rickie Fowler, Matt Kuchar and Zach Johnson. Attendance ranges from 16 to 50 depending on the venue and the players competing. It was hardly a new dynamic among American golfers.

At the 2006 Ryder Cup at the K Club outside Dublin, the American captain Tom Lehman wore a wristband engraved with the letters WWJD, standing for What Would Jesus Do? The team was accompanied to County Kildare by the PGA Tour chaplain, Larry Moody, who, some years previously had baptised Loren Roberts, Lehman's vice-captain, in the swimming pool at Disneyworld's Polynesian Resort.

Simpson, like Watson, had developed a strong faith. He had studied religion at Wake Forest University and advertises himself on Twitter as 'a sinner loved by a Savior'. At the Tour

Championship in Atlanta the week before the Ryder Cup, Simpson was spotted in a local Starbucks at 8 o'clock one morning, holding his baby and reading the Bible.

The intensity of the religious faith of men like Watson and Simpson may be unnerving to some. It may even be a source of amusement to those puzzled by, and sceptical about, such overt and public protestations of obedience to a higher force. But their beliefs were far from an irrelevance at Medinah.

Their shared faith acted as a bond for Watson and Simpson at the Ryder Cup and made them natural playing partners. In a moving elegy to his team after the competition, Davis Love made special reference to it. 'And then,' he wrote, 'there were the several times I saw Webb Simpson, the reigning US Open champion, and Bubba Watson, the Masters champion, gathering together with their wives and caddies in quiet moments of prayer and reflection. Nothing left a stronger impression on me.'

Watson, a likeable, open guy who has confessed in the past to suffering from Attention Deficit Disorder, even survived an image-bashing when a trip to the French Open in 2011 went disastrously wrong. Watson missed the cut and then the trouble really started. After a sightseeing tour of the City of Light, Watson was ridiculed for describing the wonders he saw as 'that big tower' (the Eiffel Tower), the 'building starting with an L' (the Louvre) and 'this arch I drove round in a circle' (the Arc de Triomphe).

Watson, who was born and raised in Bagdad, Florida, and paid $110,000 to buy The General Lee, the bright orange 1969 Dodge Charger driven by Lucas and Bo Duke in the *Dukes of Hazzard*, extricated himself from the mess with his usual down-to-earth charm. 'I didn't know how to pronounce the names in the right way,' Watson explained. 'That's my bad. They say it was disrespectful and I'm sorry for that. But I'm a golfer not a history major.'

Success had come relatively late for him – he was 33 when he won the Masters – but he arrived at Medinah as one of the most popular, charismatic players in the US team. Bubba Golf had worked its magic. Fans loved his wild, freewheeling style and his ability to fashion the most unlikely recoveries. They loved his populism, too, particularly the sight of him teeing off while they cheered him to the heavens.

On Friday afternoon, Watson and Simpson rode a tide of euphoria all the way to a crushing victory. Right from the first tee, right from Watson's invitation to the crowd to pump up the volume while he was taking his swing, the Americans were unstoppable. Simpson, in particular, was in the groove. He birdied the first hole to put the Americans 1 up. At the second, Watson put his ball in the water but Simpson made par and Lawrie and Hanson both missed short putts to halve the hole. America went 2 up.

On the third, Watson hit his drive 346 yards down the centre of the fairway, which drew gasps of admiration and cheers of delight from the galleries. Watson sank his birdie putt from 25 yards but this time Hanson did rescue a half with a clutch eight-footer of his own. No matter, the Americans went 3 up at the 4th even though Watson carved a wild slice into the trees off the tee.

When Watson birdied the 6th to put the Americans 4 up, it was turning into a humiliation. It felt like Lawrie and Hanson were being ground into the turf by a steamroller that would not stop. At the 7th, the Americans went 5 up. At the 8th, they went 6 up. The Europeans pulled one shot back but it was a surprise that the match lasted until the 14th hole.

But that was where it ended. Watson and Simpson sealed a

crushing 5&4 victory. They had combined for 10 birdies in 14 holes. Even the rather staid, official PGA summary called it 'ridiculous golf'. It was the most comprehensive victory of the competition so far and it moved the USA into a 3–2 lead. The momentum that Mickelson and Bradley had created was gathering force.

Watson sat down in the Media Centre with Simpson and Bradley at the end of the day and the three of them shared a few laughs. When Bradley started to get dreamy again about the shot Mickelson had hit on the 17th during their match earlier, Watson interrupted him. 'You ever see that shot that I hit that one time?' he asked Bradley with a smile.

He bristled a couple of times when journalists suggested that he was best suited to the fourballs, the inference being that there was always someone there to rescue him if Bubba Golf went rogue. 'I mean, if you look at the stats, I think I'm seventh in the world,' Watson said, 'and I think he's eighth in the world, so I think we can play golf.'

But most of all, Watson said, it had just been a blast. He even poked fun at Bradley's pre-putt mannerisms. 'He's got that weird eye,' Watson said, hamming it up for his audience and doing his best Bradley impersonation. 'Still not sure what he's looking at when he does that. Think it scares the hole, though.'

Simpson was content to play Watson's straight man, much as he had on the course. But it was clear that Love had made another fine choice of pairing when he played the two men together. Watson and Simpson had played together before at the Presidents Cup, the biennial match between the US and the rest of the world minus Europe, and now it was clear that, together with Mickelson and Bradley, they would be leading the attack on Europe.

'The key thing for us was just about having fun,' Watson said. 'You know, we are playing in the Ryder Cup. If we would have lost today, we are still playing in the Ryder Cup. So I just wanted to try to loosen up Webb, same thing I did at the Presidents Cup. It's not really about me, how I'm playing golf; it's about making Webb be the best player he can be. He's the US Open champ, obviously he knows how to play. I just made sure he was loose and he kept making birdies.'

So Watson and Simpson had flattened the opposition, Mickelson and Bradley had taken down the world number one and behind them, Dustin Johnson and Matt Kuchar, who had also been rested in the morning foursomes, were easing their way to a comfortable 3&2 victory over Justin Rose and Martin Kaymer.

That meant the Americans were 5–2 up with just Lee Westwood and rookie Nicolas Colsaerts out on the course against Woods and Stricker. The questions started coming about Olazábal's captaincy again. Why had he left out Poulter? Why had he paired Rose with Kaymer when it was obvious Rose and Poulter blended so well together?

That Friday afternoon, an air of shock settled over the European camp. They had been confident coming into the competition but now they were confronted not only by an American team that had outplayed them but which seemed to have summoned a more boisterous spirit than them.

Usually, men like Sergio García and Lee Westwood could be relied upon to get under the Americans' skin. Usually, it was their role to play the brilliant, iconoclastic, unruly kids who simply won't be silenced. Usually, it was the Europeans who were revelling in their camaraderie and sinking into reveries about the performance of their playing partner.

Now, they were busy coming to terms with the fact that the tables had been turned on them. With Poulter sitting out, the Americans had suddenly cornered the market in fist bumps and high fives. It was the Americans who were playing as a team, the Americans who were playing better than the sum of their parts.

Olazábal was worried. He knew this felt dangerous. He knew that players like Mickelson, who could usually be relied upon to under-perform, had been energized by the pairings that Love had chosen. He knew that rookies like Bradley and Simpson were playing without fear. More than that, they were playing like men who could not believe how lucky they were to be there.

Watson was doing the same. So, too, Dustin Johnson and Kuchar. It was going to be difficult to derail them. Friends and journalists were coming up to Mickelson and telling him it was the best they had ever seen him play at the Ryder Cup. They were telling him he looked like a changed man. They were telling him he looked 20 years younger all of a sudden. They were telling him he was revolutionizing his Ryder Cup record. And Mickelson was grinning from ear to ear.

'Having Keegan as a partner was a huge factor in my play,' Mickelson said. 'It was a really big deal, because he's got such great, positive energy. And when we were walking down the first hole, and I'm fifty yards ahead of our playing partner in the middle of the fairway with a little wedge, I just knew that over the course of eighteen holes, if you keep giving me wedges in the fairway, and having Keegan putt it next, we are going to be really tough to beat. And over eighteen holes, I just think that the odds are going to be in our favour.

'Keegan's just got a lot of great energy. He hits a lot of great shots and he drives the ball as well as I've ever seen a person drive it. Alternate shot (foursomes) was my favourite format because I got to hit the next shot. Best ball (fourballs), I had to play my own drive, which wasn't as fun. We made some putts and we were able to walk away with two wins over two really tough teams. We are in a good position.'

The Americans were having a ball and, for once, it was the Europeans who looked jaded and a little war-weary. For once it was the Europeans who looked as if they were struggling to rise to the occasion. It was unfair to Olazábal but it felt as if they needed some of the manic energy that a Montgomerie or a Ballesteros might bring. It felt as if they needed to step up. It felt as if the Americans were making all the running.

The European players knew it, too. Poulter had seen Bradley coming out to the first tee an hour before each session and stirring up the American supporters. He knew the value of that kind of energy and the way it could course through a team. He had heard about Watson teeing off while the crowd was cheering and yelling. He knew that someone in the European team had to step up and try to match that energy. He knew it was probably going to have to be him.

Poulter had had to watch from the sidelines while the Americans got on a roll. He understood why Olazábal had rested him and he knew that he would play twice on Saturday. He was also beginning to realize that he would have to match the four points he scored at Valhalla if Europe was going to have a chance of retaining the Ryder Cup.

He would have to energize Europe in the way Bradley and Watson had energized the US. He would have to provide the inspiration. Olazábal could only do so much. The team needed to see one of the players go toe-to-toe with the Americans on the course and reverse the momentum they had gained. It was going to be difficult. US confidence was soaring.

It was definitely not the day to try to rile any of the US team. They were cock-a-hoop. The day had gone better than they had imagined it would. They knew that they had taken their opponents by surprise with the intensity and the brilliance of their barrage. They had taken themselves by surprise. They were thrilled that one of the giants of the game, Mickelson, had responded so positively. They were feeling invulnerable.

'One of the BBC commentators today wondered how you got such a suntan because you spent so much time in the trees,' an English voice asked Mickelson in the evening. 'Would you like to comment?'

Mickelson smiled that bright, wide smile of his.

'Ah, you know we won today, right?' he said. 'I'm not sure you saw the result? Ah, you did. Okay.'

The odds were already stacked in the Americans' favour. They had won three of the four afternoon fourballs already. Now, only Westwood and a Belgian rookie stood in the way of a whitewash.

8 Europe's rookie steps up

Before Nicolas Colsaerts went to work on the afternoon of Friday 28 September, he lay at the margins of the wider sporting consciousness.

Big hitter, first Belgian ever to play in the Ryder Cup, captain's pick, reigning Volvo World Match Play Champion.

So when he arrived at Medinah he answered a questionnaire.

Which question are you asked the most? he was asked.

'Why do you keep on smoking?' he said.

What is the answer? he was asked.

'It's the only vice I have left,' he said.

Once, apparently, he had had quite a few. Once, he was on the brink of throwing it all away, of never fulfilling his potential, of wasting it on a life of partying and lack of commitment and self-doubt. He called it a 'mid-life crisis at the age of twenty-five'. What a shame it would have been if it had cost him the chance to save the Ryder Cup for Europe.

Because that is what Colsaerts did on Friday afternoon at Medinah. Pretty much single-handedly, in fact. The wags in the press room said that he was playing against Tiger Woods, Steve

Stricker and Lee Westwood that day. Technically, Westwood was his partner but the way Colsaerts played, the world number four was about as much use as a storm chaser tracking a tornado. Even he admitted that.

Poor Woods. He had stunk the place out in the morning foursomes but in the afternoon, he played like a dream. Really, it should have been his fate to crush the Europeans underfoot and lead them into a 6–2 lead at the end of the first day. On any other day, playing the way he played, whoever was up against him in the fourballs would have been swept away.

It was a fine response after he had hacked and sliced his way around the course in the morning. He had played so badly many expected Love to leave him and Stricker out in the afternoon but the captain stuck with him. Woods had a long discussion with his swing coach Sean Foley, Hank Haney's successor, in the brief break for lunch. He was desperate to make amends.

Winning on Friday afternoon would have turned Woods' Ryder Cup around. It would have made him the hero for once, the man who kept his foot on the Europeans' throat and made it well nigh impossible that they could mount a successful comeback. People would have quoted his Ryder Cup win:loss ratio a little less and his status as one of the greatest golfers ever a little more.

Woods was majestic. He carded seven birdies. If he had known that beforehand, he would surely have figured it would be enough to wipe away the memory of the earlier defeat to Ian Poulter and Justin Rose. He would have figured it would quieten the talk about his miserable Ryder Cup record. He would have figured it would have been enough to stop him being dropped for the first time in his Ryder Cup career.

There was no way he or anyone else could have anticipated that Colsaerts, a reformed party animal who was ranked

1,305th in the world only three years earlier, would produce the most extraordinary round ever by a rookie in the history of the Ryder Cup. It was the kind of round that made golf veterans sit up in their seats and rub their eyes in disbelief.

Three years ago, he had lost his playing privileges on the European Tour and fallen off the edge of the second-tier Challenge Tour. He found himself on the outside looking in, watching tournaments on television that he knew he could have been playing in, seeing those tournaments won by golfers that he knew were less talented than him.

'It was not as if I hadn't been warned,' Colsaerts said. 'I was told a million times but if you're not the one who makes the decision then it's not going to work.

'It's got to come from you. Everybody is busy doing their own thing and they don't have the time to babysit anyone.'

So Colsaerts did something about it. He checked himself into the A-Game International Golf Academy in Brisbane, Australia, which boasts that it has been 'instrumental in the development of successful tournament professionals for over 25 years'. Away from the limelight, happy in Queensland's balmy weather, Colsaerts began to prosper again. He spent three winters there.

'It was a great hideaway place for me,' he said. 'Everybody has different paths and everyone has different careers. You're going through this growing as a man sort of thing and you realize you want to be what you always dreamed of, so you've got to put your work into it, you've got to put your heart into it, and after that you become a man.'

Colsaerts fought his way back, graduating from the Challenge Tour to the main European Tour for 2010, with the help of his coach Michel Vanmeerbeek, short-game specialist Mark Roe and putting guru Dave Stockton. No wonder that when he finished his round on Friday, he took a look over his shoulder and marvelled at how far he had travelled.

'This is quite an achievement,' Colsaerts, 29, was to say after his Ryder Cup debut. 'When you look back and you see where I was three years ago, I'm just the perfect example that if you want something really bad and you put your work into it, if you've got the heart and the passion, anything is achievable. It's almost like I feel I've come back from the dead.'

No one had been quite sure how often Colsaerts would play at Medinah. Olazábal had had little doubt about making him one of his wild card picks. He left him out of the first session, figuring that foursomes would suit his game less than others, but paired him with Westwood, one of the most reliable of his team off the tee, in the afternoon fourballs. Colsaerts had been chosen as a wild card mainly because he was such a ferocious driver and that was an asset at a course as long as Medinah.

Colsaerts was the longest hitter on either team at the Ryder Cup, leading the European Tour with a driving distance average of 317.7 yards, just ahead of the 315.5 yards that Bubba Watson averages on the PGA Tour, and on Friday afternoon at Medinah, he combined power with unrelenting accuracy.

But he was not just a long hitter. He had finished tied for seventh at The Open at Royal Lytham & St Annes two months earlier, shooting a final round 65, the best of the day. And he had won the Volvo World Match Play at Casares, in Spain, a couple of months before that. He was in fine form and he loved match play.

'When you are put under the gun in a match play situation, your focus gets more intense,' Colsaerts said. 'That's why I like match play. I don't feel nervous about getting into a game and playing some guys in the Ryder Cup. I wouldn't really care who. Whoever you are drawn against and whoever you play with, it doesn't matter.'

Colsaerts and Westwood went out in the third match of the afternoon and soon the scoreboards were turning American red all around them. The matches before them and the match after them all showed the US pairings in the lead. They were surrounded. They knew Europe was under siege and that, already, the Ryder Cup odds were stacked against them.

They went one down at the first, too. Woods made a birdie with a superb 14-foot putt and the scoreboard was all red. But then Colsaerts began to play. He notched his first birdie on the 2nd, forcing Stricker to match him, halve the hole and preserve the Americans' lead. He nearly squared things up on the 3rd when another birdie putt from 15 feet took a trip around the lip of the hole before trickling back towards him.

But Colsaerts squared the match with a birdie at the 4th. Westwood was struggling to make a contribution but Colsaerts made another birdie at the 5th. Woods matched it. Another birdie from the Belgian at the 9th, his fifth on the front nine, put the Europeans ahead for the first time.

Woods made a birdie at the par-five 10th but Colsaerts, who had been playing beautifully off the tee, too, was facing a six-foot putt for an eagle. Inevitably, he sank it. Europe was now 2 up and Colsaerts was seven under after ten holes by himself. He was playing so well that it had got to the point that Westwood was standing back and laughing at his brilliance. Colsaerts was the dominant partner by such a distance that Westwood's ball only counted four times all afternoon.

Woods was barely a beat behind, though. He nailed a 25-foot putt for birdie at the 11th to bring the Americans back to within a shot of Westwood and Colsaerts. Colsaerts made his first and only bogey of the day at the 12th but responded by holing another long putt for birdie at the 13th and taking the Europeans back to 2 up. It was breathless, fantasy golf.

Colsaerts was the 35th-ranked player in the world, the lowest of any of the 24 men taking place in the Ryder Cup, but today he was playing like he was the number one. So when Woods made a birdie on the 14th to reduce the deficit to a single hole again, Colsaerts responded with yet another birdie on the 15th to restore the two-hole advantage.

Westwood remembered that moment with a grin after the round. 'I had the best seat in the house and then Nicolas brought me in to read a putt on 15 and I panicked,' Westwood said. 'I wondered why he was even asking me because everything he looked at went in. I mean, why ruin it now?'

The eyes of the golfing world were on this game now. Word had spread of the feats that Colsaerts was performing. In years to come, in the build-up to another Ryder Cup when the hype-machine is at full throttle, the score that the man from Brussels put together may simply come to be known as The Round. Westwood had moved beyond sheepishness to bemused wonder. Colsaerts said later that one of the best things about his round was seeing the expression on his face every time he turned to him after making another long putt.

The best of the drama was yet to come though. Woods hit a dramatic, beautifully judged putt on the 16th to win the hole, his sixth birdie of the round. He put his finger in the air to signify that he was back in charge. The US were just one down with two to play now and magnificently though Colsaerts had played, many wondered if he would crack under the ferocity of the onslaught from Woods.

It was at the par-three 17th where the drama got really out of hand. Woods landed his tee shot on the green and it stopped three feet from the hole. The American crowds went berserk. All the other matches were over by now and the galleries had swelled. These are the best moments in the Ryder Cup, when everything funnels down to one match.

The other players in the other matches had shaken hands and joined the throng following the duel between the master and the rookie. It was like an army following behind them. The pressure on Colsaerts off the tee at the 17th was immense and he only just cleared the water and left himself a long putt for birdie.

The Americans were exultant. They knew that the Ryder Cup was already close to being within their grasp. A 6–2 overnight lead, even with two days left to play, would be emphatic. It was hard to see any way back from that for Europe. The momentum had swung so solidly behind America that four points after one day would surely become five or six after two.

As Woods and Stricker marched on to the 17th green, there was an air of frenzied excitement around them. Fred Couples cheered loudly and gave Stricker a high-five. It felt like a formality. Unless you remembered what Tom Kite had said to Davis Love all those years ago, of course. At the Ryder Cup, expect the unexpected. At the Ryder Cup, expect your opponent to pull off the impossible shot. At the Ryder Cup, never think the hole is won until the score is on the board. So, as Woods stood contemplating a tap-in and allowed his mind to wander towards marching to the 18th tee with the match all square, Colsaerts stood over his 25-foot putt. He stroked it towards the hole and it sped firm and true straight for the centre of the hole. And then it dropped.

Woods looked at it in disbelief. Now the Europeans in the crowd went berserk. Westwood smiled the same bemused smile he had worn for most of the round. Woods holed his three-foot putt to halve the hole. Westwood and Colsaerts were guaranteed a half at least now but Westwood knew that, with all the other afternoon matches lost, it was vital that they held on to claim a victory.

The 18th was desperately tense. All four men played their second shots from the edge of the fairway, Westwood after his drive had cannoned fortuitously back into a playable lie off the boughs of a tree. Colsaerts left himself with a 22-foot putt for birdie. Woods got to within 15 feet. Colsaerts left his putt just short but close enough for the Americans to concede it for par. After Stricker had missed his putt, it left Woods with the chance to win the hole and halve the match.

Woods had already had five birdies on the back nine but this time the ball caught the left lip of the hole and rolled on. The European players and their wives, gathered around the fringes of the green, burst into celebration. First, they were applauding a quite astonishing performance from Colsaerts but they also knew that if they could regroup on Saturday, they had just grabbed a get-out-of-jail card.

Colsaerts had hit eight birdies and an eagle, the best Ryder Cup round ever by a European rookie. Woods had sunk seven birdies and still ended up on the losing team. The Americans had a 5–3 lead and the momentum, but, not for the first time over the weekend, the last match of the day gave Europe some succour. It gave them a foothold in the match. It gave them belief. It gave them a hero to applaud.

'On the eighteenth,' Colsaerts said, 'when somebody like Tiger Woods looks at you and says, "Great playing, man", you understand you have done something pretty good. I was so focused. It felt wonderful to be able to produce and deliver on such a big stage with a lot of eyes on you and this unbelievable atmosphere. I also felt very comfortable going out there with Lee.

'It was a lot of fun. I've never had so much fun and I want to have more. I dreamt about this. It was the best round I've ever played. In the circumstances, the eleven other guys I'm playing with, vital point, last game of the day, first day of Ryder Cup, my first day of Ryder Cup, then yes, this has to be my best round ever. Just don't think I'm going to putt like this every day.'

Westwood was still in a happy daze. 'You never know how people are going to react at their first round at a Ryder Cup,' he said. 'I think Nicolas took to it quite nicely. I don't know what he did Friday morning to set him off but whatever it was, I've got to find it.'

Woods was struggling to get over the disappointment of ending the day without a point but he was gracious to Colsaerts. 'I really hit it well this afternoon,' Woods said, 'but we ran into a guy who made everything today. I don't know what Nicolas shot. He was like seven under through ten. I quit counting after that. It was one of the greatest putting rounds I've ever seen.'

Woods learned after the defeat that he would be left out of the foursomes line-ups the next morning. It was momentous news. It was the first time a Ryder Cup captain had ever summoned the nerve to drop Woods even though there had been times when his form deserved it. Love was a nice guy but he showed he could make a tough decision, too.

Love knew it was a big issue. It was the first question he was asked from the floor when he came into the press conference at what had been a triumphant first day for the American team. He sought to explain Woods' absence the next morning in general strategic terms rather than as a direct response either to his poor play that morning or the fact that he had finished the day without a point.

'I've been talking to Fred Couples for well over a year about this,' Love said, 'and we just felt like we didn't want anybody to have to play five matches on this golf course. It's a big, long golf course. It's tough. And exactly what we said was going to happen happened to one of our best teams. Tiger and Steve played very well this afternoon, and just happened to get beat on the last hole by a guy who made eight birdies and an eagle.

'We just don't want guys to be worn out. We need Tiger and Steve in the afternoon tomorrow. We need Tiger and Steve on Sunday. There was a reason we sat Webb and Bubba out this morning. It was so they would be ready for the afternoon. I think Tiger needs a rest; Steve needs a rest; I need a rest.

'It's a team effort, and Tiger and Steve are very supportive friends of mine. They told me they would do whatever I asked them to do, and I can guarantee you, neither one of them are very happy about it. Not because they are sitting out but because they have to wait till tomorrow afternoon to come back from what happened to them today.'

Like a long line of American captains before him, Love found himself making excuses for Woods. Colsaerts had been hot, Woods and Stricker would have beaten any other pair out on the course except Simpson and Watson, Woods had been driving the ball very well, it was a bit cold in the morning. And so on.

Unlike many of his predecessors, though, Love had the luxury of being in charge of a team that was in the lead at the end of the first day. He had been able to drop Woods from a position of strength. And although Woods was still the highest-ranked player in the team and a man who had won 14 Majors, he was not quite in the unassailable position he had been in pre-fire hydrant.

Love could sit him out without fear of widespread expressions of astonishment. In fact, his decision brought him a good deal of praise. It made sense. It was obvious Woods carried a deep distrust of the foursomes format. It did not bring out the best in him. He was 36. He was not invincible any more. Love wanted him fresh for the Saturday fourballs and the singles on

Sunday, where he was usually strong. The decision to drop him was a smart move.

It certainly did not mask the fact that the Americans were in a strong position. It was left to Colin Montgomerie, the prophet of doom, to put the afternoon in sobering perspective. 'It was eight Americans against one European out there this afternoon and that's why it was three–one,' Montgomerie said. 'We were lucky to get away with three–one, to be honest. We have just got to get in and regroup tonight. If America can do what they have done today, we have got to do the same tomorrow. We cannot go into the singles down here. We know that ourselves and we have to win five–three tomorrow.'

Colsaerts never got close to hitting the same heights again at Medinah. Olazábal played him in every subsequent session, hoping that somehow he might be able to rediscover the magic, but he never did. His Friday afternoon fourballs performance remained there like a monument to genius, a shrine to one man's rediscovered talent.

No one who saw it will ever forget what Colsaerts did at Medinah, nor will anyone underestimate the importance of his round. It seemed as if he was playing under a spell, as if something more than skill had taken over. It left not just Woods and Westwood but everyone who saw it shaking their heads in wonder.

It was as if the effort left him spent. That was his masterpiece and nothing he did at Medinah was ever going to live up to it. He tried three times and lost three times. What a strange, capricious game golf can be. And the Americans got up the next morning and kept on rolling. As they struggled against the tide, Europe started searching for another performance like Colsaerts' that would allow them to keep believing they could work a miracle.

9 The end of restraint

When Ian Poulter and Bubba Watson arrived on the tee with their partners, Justin Rose and Webb Simpson, for the first foursomes match on Saturday morning, the crowd hailed them as if they were great demagogues come to inflame them. Golf was once about restraint but now that the Ryder Cup was in full flow and Poulter and Watson had been brought together, all restraint was gone.

This was not just a mighty collision of two of the men who best epitomized the fighting spirit of both teams, it was a match that pointed towards the future of golf. Poulter and Watson were far from the youngest men in the competition but they represented a new kind of golfer, the kind that was helping to popularize the game and open it to new markets.

More than 40,000 people thronged the course at Medinah each day during the Ryder Cup. They chugged on beer, they painted their faces red, white and blue, they cheered on their team as loudly and with as many yells of 'get in the hole' as they could and they took great delight in barracking the opposition and their shiny, happy wives and girlfriends.

This was golf but not as everybody knew it. Some felt as if an old order was passing and they mourned its vanishing. They said that being at Medinah felt more like being at an American football match, Cowboys versus Bears, or Giants versus Patriots, than a golf competition. The old etiquette was being ignored. 'Noise,' Michael Bamberger, Love's journalist confidant and defender, said, 'has won.'

In some ways, it was hard to see what made this Ryder Cup so different from many of its recent predecessors. The atmosphere at Kiawah Island in 1991 was so aggressively partisan that it was known as the War on the Shore. At Brookline in 1999, the barracking of Colin Montgomerie became so personal that his father couldn't bear to hear it.

But those who saw a change at Medinah, those who suggested we were witnessing a new direction for golf, pointed to something else. It was not just the behaviour of the fans that trampled on familiar golfing mores, it was the behaviour of the players, too.

When Watson had urged the crowd to cheer him as he was hitting his tee shot the previous afternoon, it had felt to many of those watching as though it was a seminal moment for the sport. Watson was embracing a form of progress in the game and yet he was betraying the rump of golf fans. It was like being in the crowd when Bob Dylan went electric at the Newport Folk Festival.

But now it was not just Watson urging the crowd on to cheer him as he played his shot. Now it was not just one man willing the fans to shatter the silence that is supposed to accompany a golfer playing his shot. Now it was Poulter, too. Poulter, golf's punk, golf's rabble-rouser, fist-pumper, fashion diva, high-fiver, head-banger.

Poulter had seen what Watson had done the previous afternoon and loved it. He had also realized as soon as he saw that he and Rose had been drawn against Watson and

Simpson that he would have to try to take responsibility for somehow slowing the juggernaut that Watson and Simpson and Mickelson and Bradley were driving through the European team.

And he knew that that task would begin on the first tee. It was a psychological battle, a bit like deciding how to react to the All Blacks when they perform the Haka before a match. Turn your back on them, watch passively or go right up to them and get in their face. Poulter, to no one's great surprise, chose the 'get in their face' option.

Europe was driving off first so Poulter knew what he had to do. He stepped on to the tee and urged the Europeans in the crowd to cheer. A delighted chorus of 'Ole, Ole, Ole' erupted followed by a cacophony of equally delighted boos and catcalls from the American fans. Even their boos soon turned to cheers. At the back of the tee, Watson nodded his head in approval and smiled. Everyone loved the theatre of it, including Poulter. He stepped up and smacked the ball down the fairway as the spectators screamed and cheered.

It needed someone with Poulter's confidence and front to do that. Not many in the European team would have had the appetite for it, especially not with Europe in such a parlous position. Not many would have been able to carry it off. But Poulter did it with aplomb. When he was asked later whether it had been something he planned to do or a spur of the moment reaction to the crowd, he was unequivocal.

'Well, Bubba was going to do it,' Poulter said, 'so I had to get in there first. It was a psychological tactic. He was going to do it. He's on home soil. He had all their backing so I needed our backing. I said to the boys the night before, "Don't worry, I'll have my two minutes tomorrow."'

Someone asked him whether he had been worried the ploy

might backfire, whether he would just be greeted with a chorus of American boos.

'No,' Poulter said. 'Golf fans will enjoy that stuff, they'll see it as a one-off, pretty special.'

Another question, perhaps, is whether golf fans will see it as a one-off or whether it is a form of support they will now want to replicate at The Open, the US PGA, the Tour Championship and, heaven forfend, the Masters. Again, observers like Bamberger saw significance not in the behaviour of the fans but in that of Poulter and Watson.

Bamberger called Poulter 'one half of the English rock band Poulter-Rose' and wrote that 'Saturday marked the end of civilization as we know it'. 'Poulter turned to the crowd and asked them to make noise,' Bamberger wrote. 'While he was in his pre-shot routine. And addressing the ball. And during the holy seconds while he was making his swing.

'The crowd was ridiculously amped-up, and these two emotional players gave them what they wanted. It doesn't matter whether you think it's horrible or not. Sir Nick Faldo said it was all in good fun. I think it's the further decline of golf manners, but, truly, what do I know? Life happens, and the world changes.'

Bamberger also mentioned Watson's reaction to winning the Masters the previous April and how he had wept in his mother's arms. He clearly felt the reaction had been undignified. He also felt it was not in keeping with the spirit of golf. 'The underlying point of the game's etiquette,' Bamberger wrote, 'is to put the needs of the other player ahead of your own. Even in victory.'

But Bamberger also acknowledged that part of Watson's appeal was that he did not care for the old rules. The same applied to Poulter. And even if some could dismiss their antics on the tee that Saturday morning as the kind of thing that would only ever happen at the Ryder Cup, it was hard to ignore the feeling they were indicative of wider changes happening in golf.

That is the dilemma the sport faces. Part of its appeal is that it is timeless. It is rooted in tradition. It sets great store by some of its arcane rules and its rigid honour code. Quite rightly, it takes great pride in the standards of sportsmanship it sets and the way it has remained largely immune to many of the ills (gamesmanship, match-fixing, spot-fixing, player indiscipline, lack of respect for governing bodies) that have, in one form or another, beset football, rugby and cricket.

But all sports evolve. Golf has gained and gained in popularity. It has extended its audience beyond its once-traditional catchment area. The demographic of who watches it, who spends money on it, is changing fast. It is ruled by a club called the Royal and Ancient whose name belies the acceptance that, up to a point, the sport has to move with the times.

That is what many saw happening at Medinah and they saw it most clearly that Saturday morning when Poulter and Watson went out together in the same match. They saw golf changing and Bamberger and many others like him used the occasion to put golf's evolution in a wider social context and lament the passing of something that they loved. Bamberger reminisced about the Bob Gibson era of baseball, when the crowd would watch sports matches in 'worshipful silence.' After football became the national pastime, however, things changed. The fans changed. Bamberger wrote:

> Golf's not there. Golf may be going there. The fans want to be heard. That's been true for years, in every sport. And what Bubba and Poulter are saying is that the players want to hear

them. That's certainly not true for every player, but it's true for them. It was true for John Daly. It was true for Arnold Palmer.

You're tempted to say it won't catch on, that it will never happen at the Masters. I'm not so sure. The root of the Bubba-Poulter moment is fans screaming inane things at the moment the clubface and ball meet. What Ryder Cup golf does is accelerate the trend.

Not everyone felt like Bamberger, of course. In fact, many dismissed him as a Luddite, a spokesman for the kind of country club snobbery that gives golf a bad name. Many wanted change. Many wanted a move away from a situation that exists in pockets on both sides of the Atlantic where golf clubs cling to hopelessly outmoded attitudes to issues like female membership of doggedly male-only clubs.

Many embraced the liberalization of the sport, the idea that it was being opened up to a broader cross-section of fans, that it was becoming more inclusive. Once, it had seemed that golf was an impenetrable sport, reserved for the privileged, hidden behind the imposing facades of clubhouses, out of bounds for most, too expensive for those who could not afford the clubs and the lessons. Then along comes someone like Watson, a southern boy who has never had a lesson in his life.

Perhaps we would feel the same discomfort that Bamberger felt if, say, there were seismic shifts in the behaviour of players and fans at Wimbledon. Then again, maybe we have already been through that. John McEnroe assaulted our senses when he reached the semi-finals of Wimbledon as a qualifier in 1977 and went on to embark upon a concerted challenge to the tennis authorities.

But Wimbledon learned from his rebellion and, eventually, assimilated it. It did the same with Andre Agassi a decade later.

Both men fuelled the popularity of the sport and of Wimbledon itself. The tournament may have insisted that players continued to wear predominantly white but it accepted many criticisms and acted on them. It put a roof on Centre Court, it accepted the use of new technology to assist in the making of line calls. It changed with the times.

Sure, there was still silence when the players served and quiet was still encouraged during rallies. But tennis was a broad church. At the US Open there is a low hum of continual chatter during points, a bit like at a baseball game. The French Open at Roland Garros is somewhere in between. Tennis thrived in each different theatre.

Cricket is attempting something different with Twenty20, with a reasonable degree of success. The Ryder Cup is not the same because it was not developed specifically to meet a perceived need or chime with an audience that was perceived to have a shorter attention span. But in some ways, and more successfully, the Ryder Cup performs the same function for golf.

And despite the reservations of men like Bamberger, golf is the better for it. The old reserve and the familiar etiquette are not being swept away, not at the Masters and The Open anyway. The supporters who flock to Augusta and British links courses respect the traditions that are upheld there and they know that at Augusta in particular, if they do not respect them, they will be ejected from the grounds with a minimum of warning and an absence of regret.

Golf, like tennis, like cricket, has room for more than one code of behaviour. It has developed the flexibility to allow fans and players to act in different ways at different tournaments and competitions. The Ryder Cup is different. Everyone accepts that. But there is no reason why its shade of difference should be more powerful than The Open's, say. There is no reason why it should lead golf down the road to Hell, to the place traditionalists like Bamberger see in his nightmares where golf fans brawl in the streets and urinate in sinks.

What Watson and Poulter symbolized at Medinah was not the funeral of golf etiquette but a sign that the sport was capable of evolving to appeal to a new generation of fans. To most of the sport's fans, it felt like an overwhelmingly positive sign, an intoxicating moment in the sport's history. Golf was madly popular. Watson and Poulter were players and characters who appealed to a younger audience. Golf was not just surviving. It was thriving. There was nothing to mourn here but there was an awful lot to celebrate.

Even though it was 7.20 a.m., even though it was a bitterly cold morning under the clear skies of a Midwest fall, Poulter and Watson teed off against a background of frenzied excitement and wild cheering. Poulter's drive came to rest in a bunker. Watson's huge tee-shot carried the bunker. They marched off down the fairway, Watson high-fiving everyone he could reach, to great roars of encouragement.

Olazábal had sent Poulter and Rose out first because it already looked as if they were his strongest pairing and he knew that he needed to halt the American momentum. He also knew that Poulter would revel in the scenario that he had been presented with, the opportunity to lead his team into battle against the odds and in the face of a hostile crowd.

Davis Love III had adopted the same policy with Watson and Simpson. Mickelson and Bradley had emerged as his strongest pairing but Love felt that he could afford to put them out second and let Watson and Simpson, who had played beautifully as Watson's straight man the previous afternoon, set the tone early.

Rose was being overshadowed by Poulter. That was inevit-able. But the two men had been great friends for a long time and Rose was crucial to keeping Poulter focused. Shy, reserved and courteous, Rose was the opposite of the confident, brash extrovert who was his partner, which was one of the main reasons they played together and got on together so well.

So even though Poulter had taken the weight on his shoulders on the first tee and urged the crowd to do their worst, he had hit his tee-shot into the bunker and it fell to Rose to try to rescue the situation. He did it superbly, lifting the ball out of the sand and leaving it seven feet from the pin. Watson missed the Americans' putt for birdie from the back of the green, but Poulter rolled his into the cup. The rock band Poulter-Rose were 1 up after one.

Simpson fluffed a golden opportunity to strike back when missing a tiny putt on the 2nd, but the Americans immediately had another chance to hit back on the next. Watson's tee shot was 65 yards longer than Poulter's and Simpson stuck the American approach to within three feet of the hole. The Europeans conceded the birdie and when Poulter missed his birdie attempt from 18 feet, the match was all square.

Another huge drive from Watson on the fifth gave America the advantage again. Simpson was able to carry the bunker at the front of the green to leave Watson with a 40-foot putt for eagle. The Europeans could only manage a par, which left Watson and Simpson with two putts to win the hole. Watson rolled his effort to within three feet and Simpson tapped in to put the US 1 up.

At the 9th, though, Watson crashed his drive deep into the trees while Poulter's 294-yard tee-shot went right down the middle of the fairway. Simpson tried to rescue the situation by lifting his ball over a tree but it landed in a greenside bunker and the Europeans were in control. Watson put his bunker shot four feet past the hole leaving Poulter with a putt for birdie to bring the match level again. It was seven feet downhill, left to right. Poulter gave it a nudge and watched it roll. It went dead centre of the cup and Poulter celebrated with a fist-pump. It was the first hole the Europeans had won since the opening hole.

At the par-five 10th, Europe went back into the lead. It was an untidy hole. Rose's tee-shot was in the rough and Poulter, blocked by a tree, could only squirt it back out on to the fairway. Simpson's drive was down the middle of the fairway but Watson's second went wide right. Both teams had long putts for birdie. Watson's rolled seven feet past the hole, Poulter's was only two feet short. Simpson conceded the par and then missed his attempt to halve the hole. The match had turned around. Europe was 1 up.

By now, it was clear which way the matches behind them were going. Poulter and Rose saw a lot of American red on the scoreboards. They heard a lot of wild roars coming from all around them, roars that were way too loud to be greeting triumphs for European golfers. Europe's situation was getting worse. It looked as if the gap between the two teams was widening.

By now, Captain Love, already sensing that Poulter and Rose would form the most obdurate element of the European resistance, had joined the crowds following the match, but at the 11th he witnessed Poulter at his best. Under pressure, needing a six-foot birdie putt to halve the hole and keep Europe in the lead, Poulter drained it, let out a scream of triumph and pounded his chest with his fist. Europe's heart was still beating.

Now the Americans began to feel the heat. They played the 12th badly. Simpson duck-hooked his drive and Watson's recovery attempt came very close to ending up in the water. Simpson fluffed the next shot, too, trying to loft a flop-shot high over the bank leading up to the green but failing to make it over the ridge. It landed on the downslope and rolled back close to Simpson's feet.

Poulter, whose shocking, hooked second shot was brilliantly recovered by Rose inches from the edge of the lake, was left with a 10-foot par putt to win the hole and increase Europe's lead. He made it. He pumped his fist for all he was worth this time, screaming 'come on' and gesturing at the Europeans in the crowd to turn up the volume. Once again, his defiance was turning into Europe's greatest strength. He and Rose were now 2 up.

The next three holes were halved and it began to seem as if Poulter and Rose were cruising towards their point. But at the par-four 16th, the match changed again. Rose missed the fairway to the right with his drive. Simpson missed it to the left. Poulter next. He missed the green to the right. Watson put his approach in the bunker. Rose took an age to play his shot, walking up the steep slope that led to the green, pondering his plan. The plan backfired. The ball dropped short and did not clear the rough.

Simpson's bunker shot went 13 feet past the hole but Poulter's chip was poor and he left the ball five feet short. That left Watson with a putt to win the hole but he missed it left. Rose conceded the putt for Simpson and faced a bogey putt of his own to halve the hole. He missed it right. Europe's lead was cut to one hole with two to play.

At the spectacular 17th, it fell to Watson and Poulter to hit high-pressure tee-shots over the water and on to the green. Both managed it and both were subsequently left with short putts for par. Both holed them. Europe were 1 up with one hole to play. They were guaranteed half a point but they knew from the scoreboards that that would not be enough. They could not afford to lose the 18th.

Simpson found the middle of the fairway but Rose's three-wood went into the left rough. Watson hit a masterful second shot to within eight feet of the hole and Poulter called Rose over to discuss his yardage and club selection. It was the most important shot of the morning so far and Poulter landed it on the front right of the green, leaving Rose with a 35-foot putt for birdie.

Rose judged it beautifully but left it a foot short, close enough for the Americans to concede the par. Simpson had an eight-foot downhill putt to win the hole and halve the match. It was another of the moments which both teams looked back on at the end of the competition and saw a point at which the Cup could have been won. If Simpson had holed the putt and Europe had not managed to win a single match all morning, it would have been a devastating blow to European morale.

But Simpson had not played nearly as well that Saturday morning as he had the previous afternoon. He had been strug-gling with the putter. So when he stood over the ball on the 18th, there was hope for the Europeans. Watson stood over the putt with him, helping with the read. He even pointed to a spot between ball and hole that he thought Simpson should aim for. Simpson dribbled it towards the hole but it just slid past to the left. Poulter and Rose had their point.

The Americans had shot two over as a team, the Europeans level par. It was far from vintage stuff and Watson and Simpson had played well below the exalted standards they had reached the day before. But Poulter and Rose had done what they had to do. They had ground out a win. They had given Europe a foothold in the competition.

'I feel like that was a good point for us,' Poulter said. 'We actually didn't have our best stuff today and to win that point was massive. It was a difficult game psychologically. Bubba is Bubba. He was pretty special yesterday and Ian and I talked about it last night. We knew he was going to get the crowd to cheer as he was hitting again today so why not stand there and enjoy the fun of what it was? My heart rate went from, I would say, one hundred to one hundred and eighty pretty quickly, but I mean, it was a great buzz for sure.'

Watson, for once, was deflated. He had played well but admitted the rhythm of foursomes had left him uncomfortable. 'We just kept missing putts. We could never get any momentum going our way. They were holing putts, they were playing great golf, and they just beat us. It's hard to get in a rhythm playing every other shot.'

If Watson was deflated, most of the fans lucky enough to be packed into Medinah that morning were drunk on what they had seen. Golf played in a great spirit, played with verve and a beguiling mixture of abandon and precision. It had been a great sporting spectacle.

Chicago resident Luke Donald chats to Chicago Bulls basketball legend and golf fanatic Michael Jordan.

US captain Davis Love III directing operations as his team begins to dominate Europe.

Brandt Snedeker and Jim Furyk take stock on the last green during their narrow victory over Rory McIlroy and Graeme McDowell .

Main picture: A huge gallery gathers around the redesigned 15th green as the Americans press their advantage.

Left: Webb Simpson holds his head in despair as his missed birdie putt hands a foursomes victory to Poulter and Rose.

Below: Poulter is congratulated by Simpson but his victory with Rose over Simpson and Watson was the only point gained by Europe in the third session.

ANDREW REDINGTON/GETTY IMAGES

MIKE EHRMANN/GETTY IMAGES

POULTER

Former US president George W. Bush stretches to shake hands with a spectator on Saturday afternoon after sharing a golf buggy with Captain Love.

Olazábal feels the Ryder Cup slipping away as the Americans race into a commanding lead.

Matt Kuchar celebrates a birdie as he and Dustin Johnson beat Nicolas Colsaerts and Paul Lawrie.

Luke Donald began to return to form on Saturday afternoon as he and García fought to a crucial victory over Woods and Stricker.

Simpson and Watson celebrate after crushing Rose and Francesco Molinari 5&4.

ANDREW REDINGTON/GETTY IMAGES

Poulter pumps himself up to the limit on the 17th late on Saturday afternoon in the midst of a run of five birdies in a row that allowed him and Rory McIlroy to beat Jason Dufner and Zach Johnson, and give Europe faint hope that all was not yet lost.

ANDY LYONS/GETTY IMAGES

A message of defiance from Paddy Power's Skytext early on Sunday morning. Outside the inner confines of the European team, no one really believed it.

Every European player took an image of Ballesteros with them on the sleeve of their jumper when they went out on the course.

A silhouette of Ballesteros's most famous winning pose also appeared on every European's golf bag.

Lee Westwood celebrates his winning putt in the singles against Matt Kuchar on the 16th. He later admitted to 'shaking like a leaf' while he stood over it.

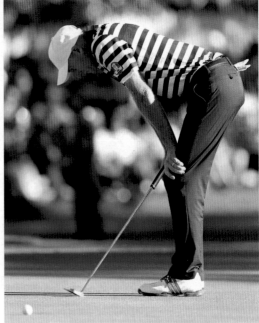

Jim Furyk provides the most poignant images at Medinah when he bends over as if winded in the moment of his defeat to Sergio García.

10

Phil's team

It fell to Lee Westwood and Luke Donald to try to stop the freight train. Drawn against Phil Mickelson and Keegan Bradley, it was not long before they had to jump out of the way and let it roar onwards. Ian Poulter and Justin Rose made their show of defiance but now the Americans were sweeping all before them.

Westwood seemed out of sorts at Medinah. Perhaps that was a harsh judgement, a product of setting his performance against the excellence of some of his previous Ryder Cup experiences. Usually, he was the life and soul of the team but this time he appeared curiously flat and stripped of inspiration.

Westwood had been in good form coming into the competition. He had not been in contention at the Tour Championship the week before but he finished joint runner-up to Rory McIlroy at the BMW Championship at Crooked Stick at the start of September and had tied for fifth at The Barclays at Bethpage Black, outside New York, at the end of August.

Some believed that the burden of going another year without winning a Major was beginning to weigh heavily upon him. He had finished third at the US Masters in April after leading after the first round and closing strongly to within two shots of play-off winner Bubba Watson.

He had also carded a top-ten finish at the US Open but finished well off the pace at The Open at Royal Lytham & St Annes and failed to make the cut at the PGA, his 59th appearance in a Major championship. He will be 40 in 2013. Time is running out for him to get the win his career and his consistency deserve.

Westwood has one of the driest senses of humour on tour but even he is beginning to get bored of the questions about whether he will be unfulfilled if he fails to win one of the titles that the best golfers measure themselves by. Everyone knows what the answer to that question is really so there is little point in continuing to ask it.

Frustration about that gap in his CV took its toll after his disappointment at the PGA, though. One of the recurring themes of his near misses in Majors has been the weakness of his short game compared to his strength off the tee and after he missed the cut at the Ocean Course, it was announced that he had split with his long-term coach, Pete Cowen.

'Lee needs to try something different with his chipping and putting,' his manager, Chubby Chandler, said. 'He's never been the greatest chipper, but his putting also needs work. He knows that. Parting company with Pete is because he's passing on advice to Lee but he's not around to follow it through.

'Lee is very structured about going to the gym, but not about practising so when Graeme McDowell and Pete's other players are booking him, Lee is leaving it late and is having to work around them. Pete was at Kiawah for two days with Graeme this week when Lee wanted to work with him, so it just wasn't working out. Lee's the sort who needs someone standing over him, making him hit chip after chip and telling him what he's doing wrong. It's not like he's got the yips or anything – he just needs to improve his technique.

'When you miss the cut after that, it gets even more frustrating, and that probably brought matters to a head. And Lee admits he needed to shake things up because he'd lost his focus and his enthusiasm a bit, because he wasn't getting the rewards for his long game.'

Westwood has still had an outstanding career. He has had spells as the world's number one and he has been one of Europe's best performers in the Ryder Cup.

Medinah was his eighth appearance in the Ryder Cup and he was already one of the greats of the competition, winning 8½ points at Oakland Hills and the K Club and equalling Arnold Palmer's record of 12 matches unbeaten when he halved his first two outings at Valhalla in 2008.

When he arrived at Medinah, he was sixth on the all-time list of European points scorers in the competition. Only Nick Faldo, Bernhard Langer, Colin Montgomerie, Seve Ballesteros and José María Olazábal had scored more. 'I've got nineteen points and I hope to play in several more Ryder Cups and win many more points,' Westwood said before he arrived in Chicago. 'Faldo holds the record with twenty-five points and it's certainly a goal of mine to become the top scorer. You've always got to have ambitions in this game, and that one is right up there.'

Overtaking Faldo would taste particularly sweet for Westwood, too. At Valhalla, he was responsible for Westwood's most dismal performance in the Ryder Cup when he underlined his reputation as Captain Cock-up by taking the bizarre decision to inform Westwood on the 10th tee of a finely balanced Friday afternoon fourball match that he was being dropped from the Saturday morning foursomes.

Bearing in mind Westwood had not lost a match in the competition for six years and was on the verge of equalling

Palmer's record, it was the kind of call that only a man as self-obsessed as Faldo could make. Westwood had never been left out of a session before and if Faldo hoped the news would somehow motivate him, it had the opposite effect.

'That was my lowest point in the Ryder Cup,' Westwood said. 'Easily. It was the only match I have ever missed. We were two up going down ten. What happened happened. We ended up halving but that was twelve matches without defeat for me. Seemed a strange time to drop somebody to me.

'I would say it is very difficult for a captain to have a significant effect on you winning a Ryder Cup but they can have a significant effect on you losing it if they get the little things wrong. We all know the job we are there for, what we have got to do to win it, but that can be made easier by the little things that the captains do.'

Westwood had not had the best start to the competition at Medinah. Many had been puzzled that he was paired with Francesco Molinari in the Friday morning foursomes and the plan didn't work. They were comprehensively outplayed by Jason Dufner and Zach Johnson. In the afternoon fourballs, he was a spectator as Colsaerts went on the rampage and beat Tiger Woods and Steve Stricker by himself. Westwood was suffering from being a player who Olazábal felt he could pair with anybody rather than tying him to a favoured partner. He had enjoyed some of his finest moments in the competition alongside Sergio García but Olazábal kept them apart at Medinah and, on Saturday morning, it was Donald who lined up with him against Mickelson and Bradley.

Bradley had already paid one visit to the first tee that morning. Warming up on the practice putting green while it was still dark, he had heard the crowd chanting and decided to dash over the footbridge to give himself an extra shot of adrenalin. He whirled his arms and worked them into a frenzy just like he had the day before and then returned to his putting.

Mickelson gave him a pep talk before play began. He reminded Bradley that they were coming up against players who were ranked number three and number four in the world. He reminded him about Westwood's Ryder Cup record. He reminded him that until the previous day, Donald had gone seven matches unbeaten in foursomes. He reminded him that both Westwood and Donald had been world number one within the last 16 months.

So Mickelson gave the lecture and then he began the demonstration. After a monster drive from Bradley at the opening hole, Mickelson put his approach to within a foot of the pin. The Europeans conceded the birdie, then Donald missed a seven-foot putt to halve the hole. A few minutes into the match and the Americans were already on a roll, already high-fiving, already congratulating each other, already revelling in the fun they were having.

On the 2nd Mickelson hit his tee-shot to within 12 feet of the hole. Westwood pulled his into the water and then, after Donald had lofted an approach from the drop-zone, Westwood missed a putt for bogey. There was no need for the Americans to putt again. They were 2 up after two.

Westwood was struggling. His tee-shot at the 4th found the rough, his next shot was a misjudged chip. Europe escaped with a half but only just. Donald was struggling, too. He dumped his drive on the 5th into a fairway bunker, leaving Westwood no choice but to lay up. The Americans birdied the hole and Westwood responded with a clutch putt of his own for a half. It was the highlight of the Europeans' round.

The Americans were back in their hyperactive, backslapping groove. Bradley's idiosyncratic build-up to every shot had not been diluted. He still walked up to the ball, danced backwards, then did a little hop and skip towards it before settling on his address. It is something golf fans are going to have get used to because Bradley is not particularly keen to change it.

'I kind of equate it to a tennis player getting ready to receive a serve, how they're kind of bouncing around,' Bradley said. 'I can't just stand there and look at the shot. It's kind of like when you're about ready to receive a serve in tennis and they're kind of hopping around back there, just trying to not stay still.

'And I realize it's very strange and it's very awkward and it's way different than everybody else. But that's kind of what I do. It's a way for me to stay athletic and not stagnant. Any time somebody does something that's drastically different, it's going to cause some weird reactions. But for me, it's always been something that I've done and I feel comfortable doing.'

However different it was, it was working just fine for Bradley at Medinah. At the par-four 6th, the US went 3 up when Donald's eight-foot putt for par to halve the hole lipped out. Now the Americans turned the screw. Mickelson hit the second shot on the par-five 7th to within 15 feet of the hole, leaving Bradley a putt for eagle with the Europeans off the green.

Donald played a poor third, leaving it short of the green in the bunker. Westwood's attempt at recovery didn't work either. He ran his shot from the sand 25 feet past the hole. The match was fast turning into a rout. Mickelson was left with a two-foot putt for birdie to win the hole and rolled it in. The Americans were 4 up.

After a brief respite for the Europeans with a halved hole at the 8th, the agony continued at the next. Bradley smoked his drive over the trees and left Mickelson with a 100-yard wedge to the hole. He hit it to within eight feet, Donald missed his birdie attempt from 20 feet and then Bradley sank his putt. He celebrated as if he had won another Major, whooping and yelling and punching the air. The Americans were unrelenting. They were now 5 up at the turn.

It meant that Mickelson and Bradley had posted 19 birdies in their last 41 holes. They were playing irresistible golf. At the par-five 10th, they were on the green in two again. Donald attempted to lay up with Europe's second shot. The problem was he laid up into a fairway bunker. It summed up the way the Europeans were playing. Donald nearly rescued a half with a 20-foot birdie putt but it turned sharply right just when he thought he had salvaged a little dignity. The US were now 6 up after 10.

The Americans might easily have gone dormie on the 11th but Bradley missed a 10-footer and the inevitable was postponed for another hole. Up ahead, Watson and Simpson were engaged in their battle with Poulter and Rose and there was a delay in the second game while Watson attempted to extricate himself from the woods.

Mickelson hit a poor drive on the 12th but even though his shot cannoned off the branches of a tree, Bradley made a decent recovery. Mickelson produced another shot of genius next, hitting a stupendous wedge that landed 20 feet from the cup and rolled and rolled down the slope. It came to a halt a few inches from the hole. The Europeans conceded par.

Westwood had a 30-foot putt to win the hole. He left it five feet short. Donald stood over the ball. He had long been considered the best putter in the European team. He was third in the PGA's Strokes Gained Putting table for 2012. Only Brandt Snedeker among the Ryder Cup players was higher. Donald needed to make the putt to extend the game to the 13th hole. He pushed it right.

Mickelson and Bradley had won 7&6. It was one of the

biggest winning margins in Ryder Cup history. The biggest winning margin in an 18-hole fourball match was 7&5, recorded in 1981 at Walton Heath when the American duo of Lee Trevino and Jerry Pate defeated the British pair of Nick Faldo and Sam Torrance.

Unfortunately for Westwood and Donald, they had matched the record for the worst ever foursomes defeat. Two other European pairs shared their fate. Ken Brown and Des Smyth were beaten 7&6 by Hale Irwin and Tom Kite at The Greenbrier in 1979 and Faldo and David Gilford lost by the same score to Paul Azinger and Mark O'Meara at Kiawah Island in 1991.

Donald and Westwood were, not surprisingly, keen to keep their comments to a minimum after the match. 'Well, it was tough, yeah,' Donald said. 'Phil is a good partner to Keegan. He's obviously been a rock star this week and they did nothing wrong. They played extremely solid. We didn't quite have our games this morning, and we just couldn't quite get the momentum on our side. We just kept pushing and trying as hard as we could, but they kept coming up with great shots.'

It was a brutal defeat for Europe at a difficult time. They needed to try to claw back momentum after the events of Friday but the emphatic nature of the Americans' victory was another blow to morale. It added to the feeling that the US were having a great big party, playing without pressure, enjoying each other's company, waltzing towards triumph.

'I think Keegan and I have gelled as well as any American pairing ever has in this competition,' Mickelson said. 'The European side has had some great teammates with Seve and Ollie and some others, but to be able to share this experience with Keegan and to partake in his great play and experience the Ryder Cup together has been really awesome. We've had so much fun. The crowd has provided so much energy, and it's brought our best golf out.'

There was one consolation for Europe, although it seemed like cold comfort at the time. Mickelson hinted soon after the match that he and Bradley would sit out the afternoon four-balls session. There was widespread disbelief among the American media about that but Mickelson seemed to be fully behind the idea.

'The thing about it is,' Mickelson said, 'historically and mathematically, the guys that have played five matches have not done as well in the singles and we want to make sure we're rested and focused on the singles. We've got a lot of guys on this team that are playing some great golf who need to get out and play as well, and don't be surprised if we end up not playing because we don't want to risk two points for one.'

At the time, it did not seem as if Love was taking too much of a risk. The US was in complete command and strengthening its grip on the competition all the time. Love was attempting to take a scientific approach to his captaincy and the statistical research told him, as Mickelson said, that players who played five matches became more vulnerable in the latter stages.

Love was confident that his team was deep enough in terms of talent and players in form that he could afford to rest even a pair like Mickelson and Bradley who were sweeping all before them. The way they were playing, it seemed they would be guaranteed another point on Saturday afternoon if Love played them, but the US captain would not be swayed.

Afterwards, Mickelson said he had spoken to Love on the 10th hole of the match against Westwood and Donald, when he and Bradley were at their most dominant, and urged him not to reconsider his plan to rest them in the afternoon. He said that he and Bradley would be emotionally spent. His instinct conformed to the story that Love's statistics were telling him.

Love's critics argued after the competition that he had been too rigid. They said that captaincy should be about adapting to circumstances and that Love should have responded to how Mickelson and Bradley were playing and ignored his statistical analysis. They said his decision was a sign of complacency and that it was the single biggest mistake that contributed to throwing the Ryder Cup away.

It was a harsh judgement. Despite the brilliance of their play in the first three sessions, there is no guarantee that Mickelson and Bradley would have reproduced it in a fourth. In a football tournament, a manager will often rest one or two of his best players if he gets a chance to try to keep them fresh for a match that matters more. That is exactly what Love was doing.

At the time, it seemed like smart, mature, authoritative captaincy. It seemed as though Love was staying level, determined to extract the most from a rich seam of playing resources. He could not have known that the Ryder Cup would take such an extraordinary turn that gambling on Mickelson and Bradley winning one last precious point on Saturday afternoon would have been a risk worth taking.

11 Blood in the water

José María Olazábal had sent Ian Poulter out in the first match on Saturday morning and Rory McIlroy in the last. His attack dog and his best player bookending the fightback. That was his idea. Poulter had done his bit. He and Justin Rose had fought their way to a win. Now Olazábal needed McIlroy to bring the team home and ensure that Europe did not fall any further behind before the afternoon fourballs.

Lee Westwood and Luke Donald had been humiliated by Phil Mickelson and Keegan Bradley and, in the next match, Nicolas Colsaerts and Sergio García could never quite get ahead of Jason Dufner and Zach Johnson. Colsaerts had been unable to rediscover the genius that had infused his game the previous afternoon and when he hit a six-iron off the tee and into the water at the 17th, it sealed a 2&1 defeat for him and García.

That left Europe staring at a 7–4 deficit. By mid-morning, the Ryder Cup had almost ceased to feel like a competition. It was veering towards the atmosphere you get at a parade or a party. The tension was going out of it. It was beginning to feel like a sure thing. It was becoming a celebration of the rebirth of American golf and the demise of Europe.

But McIlroy was still out there with Graeme McDowell,

locked in another tense struggle with Jim Furyk and Brandt Snedeker, who they had beaten on the last hole the previous morning. Olazábal desperately needed the two Northern Irishmen to secure a repeat of that result now that things had turned so decisively against Europe.

McIlroy and McDowell had been touted as Europe's leading pair before the Ryder Cup began. Everyone knew they would play together. They were firm friends, compatriots and brilliant players. McIlroy was the world number one and the winner of the most recent Major, the PGA Championship. McDowell was the 2010 US Open champion, the hero of the last Ryder Cup at Celtic Manor and had come desperately close to winning The Open at Royal Lytham & St Annes a few months before Medinah.

But neither had played as well as they could on the opening day. The US had been determined to target McIlroy with their best players and try and dent Europe's confidence by wounding their star. They had achieved that on Friday afternoon when Mickelson and Bradley had beaten them 2&1 in the fourballs.

The pressure was on McIlroy to deliver now. His team desperately needed him to lead them in the face of the American onslaught. He had been in brilliant form coming into the Ryder Cup. He had won the PGA at the beginning of August, and then the Deutsche Bank and BMW Championships back to back at the beginning of September.

He seemed relaxed and happy when he arrived in Chicago, although an exchange on the Wednesday before the competition started with the *Daily Mail*'s brilliant sports diarist, Charlie Sale, appeared to rattle him.

'You're moving to Florida,' Sale said, 'but you're selling up your house in Northern Ireland, and obviously you can well afford to have houses on both sides of the Atlantic.'

'I never said I was moving to Florida,' McIlroy said.

'But you're selling up in Northern Ireland, though?' Sale persisted.

'I am, yeah.'

'Can you say why you don't want to keep a base over there?'

'Doesn't make financial sense. I don't spend enough time at home to warrant the running costs of a home like that and the practice facility.'

McIlroy had been amiable and assured in his press conference until that point. After the exchange, his attitude changed and his answers became more clipped and curt. Some worried that a controversy that had been stirred up about a conflict in his golfing allegiances to Britain and Ireland a few weeks earlier was still preying on his mind.

Everyone who knows McIlroy speaks of an honest, down-to-earth, decent man who has stayed remarkably grounded despite his ascent to fame and fortune. And when he was asked by the *Daily Mail*'s respected golf correspondent, Derek Lawrenson, about golf being part of the 2016 Olympics in Rio and who McIlroy would choose to represent, he answered openly.

'What makes it such an awful position to be in,' McIlroy said, 'is I have grown up my whole life playing for Ireland under the Golfing Union of Ireland umbrella but the fact is, I've always felt more British than Irish. Maybe it was the way I was brought up, I don't know, but I have always felt more of a connection with the UK than with Ireland. And so I have to weigh that up against the fact that I've always played for Ireland and so it is tough. Whatever I do, I know my decision is going to upset some people but I just hope the vast majority will understand.'

In some ways, McIlroy's comments were a logical extension

of his upbringing. He had grown up in Holywood, County Down, just outside Belfast. North Down is arguably the most British part of Northern Ireland, not in an overtly sectarian, murals on the walls type of way but in a comfortable, middle-class way. He comes from a 'soft Unionist' background.

McIlroy supports the Ulster rugby team and loves Manchester United. He is not political at all. In fact, he is apolitical but most people in North Down consider themselves more British than Irish. McIlroy was just articulating the echoes from his youth.

Some of the signs of his allegiance were already there anyway. There is footage on YouTube that purports to show him throwing an Irish tricolour to the ground when it was offered to him in the immediate aftermath of his US Open victory last year. There is no evidence McIlroy actively threw it to the ground but when it was thrown to him, he certainly did not grab it and wrap it round his shoulders. In contrast, he has been pictured celebrating victories with the Ulster flag.

Predictably, perhaps, his comments in the *Mail* caused a furore in Ireland and, a few days later, McIlroy was forced to publish a long letter via his Twitter account which elaborated on his position, although he made it plain he considered the need for such an explanation a regrettable distraction. The letter bemoaned the fact that, rather than McIlroy's recent golfing successes being a more popular topic of conversation, the issue of his cultural identity – and therefore his allegiance ahead of the 2016 Rio Olympics – had re-emerged. McIlroy reiterated that he is a proud Ulsterman and that he values support from both his British and Irish fans, and clarified that he had not yet made a decision on his participation in the 2016 Olympics, choosing to concentrate on his golfing prowess and focusing on winning Major Championships.

The letter brought a temporary end to the issue but McIlroy's reaction to Charlie Sale's question about his house move suggested that, understandably, he was wary of reigniting it during the Ryder Cup. As he and McDowell, both proud Northern Irishmen, stood on the first tee on Saturday morning, they did not have to worry about Britain or Ireland. They were Europeans but they were Europeans with a mountain to climb.

They went 1 down straight away. McDowell began as he had done the previous morning, hooking his drive off the tee. He missed the lower branches of the oak on the left of the fairway this time but found a bunker instead. McIlroy seemed to have rescued the situation by hitting to within 10 feet of the flag from the sand but Snedeker's approach got slightly closer. McDowell slid his birdie putt right. Furyk drained his. The Europeans were behind.

Furyk missed another birdie putt to win the hole on the second after a fine tee shot over the lake from Snedeker and the Europeans hung in there. The weather, for a second successive day, was crisp and clear and McIlroy and McDowell chatted happily all the way from tee to green under blue skies. Up above, stunt pilots commissioned by the bookmaker Paddy Power were writing messages in the heavens encouraging the European team and goading the Americans. The Northern Irishmen halved the hole but as they walked to the 4th they could see the entire scoreboard was American red.

At the 5th, the Europeans had a chance to level the match. Furyk missed the fairway with his drive and Snedeker could only punch it back out from a poor lie. McDowell and McIlroy were on the edge of the green in two but McDowell's bump and run came to rest 20 feet from the hole. McIlroy grimaced and shook his head when he missed the putt for birdie. He knew Furyk's third shot had left Snedeker, the hottest putter on the tour, with a chance to win the hole. Snedeker took the chance. The US were 2 up after five holes.

Furyk made a 10-foot par putt to halve the 6th and as McIlroy and McDowell walked down the 7th fairway they gazed skywards again. 'Rory's Gonna Getcha,' the white-on-blue message read. McIlroy smiled. In the afternoon, the sky writers were to turn their attention to trying to upset the American team. 'Tiger Loves a Bit of Rough,' the stunt pilots wrote. Captain Love was not amused.

McIlroy had a chance to win the 7th but his relatively straightforward birdie putt lipped out and his smile was a memory. Another one had got away. On the 8th, though, they finally got a hole back, making an eighth successive par after a poor second shot from Furyk had left Snedeker needing to chip in to try to halve the hole. Europe was 1 down.

The 9th and 10th were halved but on the 11th the momentum shifted back towards the US when McDowell missed a birdie chance and Furyk made his. It was one of the match's big turning points. Having battled their way back into it, McIlroy and McDowell now knew they faced a tough fight to get two shots back in seven holes against a pair determined to avenge their defeat the previous day.

By now, the Europeans could see that Westwood and Donald had been obliterated and that Colsaerts and García were struggling. They knew they had to try to squeeze something out of the match but McIlroy missed a makeable birdie on the 12th and Furyk and Snedeker were one hole closer to victory.

The Europeans were playing solidly. They recorded their 13th consecutive par at the next hole. But they were not putting well enough to put the Americans under real pressure. McIlroy did produce a stunning chip from 50 yards on the 14th that rolled to within a few inches of the hole and was close enough for the Americans to concede. But Furyk, who was playing superbly, rolled in from six feet to claim the half.

Neither team took on the 15th, both electing to lay up. It was a surprise that the Europeans did not go for it. They had little to lose by now although McDowell's shot into the water there the previous day may have weighed heavily on his mind as he stood on the tee. Another hole was halved. The Americans were one step closer to another morale-boosting victory.

But at the 16th, McIlroy finally made a birdie, the Europeans' first of the round and they brought themselves to within one hole of the Americans with two holes left to play. Perhaps not taking a risk on the 15th would pay off after all. And now McDowell went for it. His tee shot at the par-three 17th was right at the hole. The Americans said all week that McDowell had ice in his veins and now he was proving it. When Snedeker just missed his long birdie putt, McIlroy had a fine chance to take the match all square going to the last. But his 10-foot uphill putt missed left by a fraction. McIlroy hung his head.

Europe had to win the 18th to salvage a half from the match. They knew by now that Westwood and Donald and Colsaerts and García had both lost. They knew how crucial half a point here could be. McIlroy responded. He crushed his drive up the centre of the fairway. But McDowell frowned after he hit his approach and swished his club through the air in anger. His ball shot through the back of the green. Meanwhile, Snedeker was bunkered off the tee and Furyk, after taking an age deciding what to do, found the front of the green from the sand with an excellent shot.

McIlroy, who is a genius from this range, clipped his putt towards the hole but it slid a few inches past on the right-hand side, eliciting another grimace from the world number one.

That meant the Americans needed only to two-putt to halve the hole and win the match. Snedeker rolled his putt close. The Americans looked at McIlroy and McDowell to see if they would concede. Furyk began to line up the putt but then the Northern Irishmen bowed to the inevitable. They conceded. The Americans had won their third point of the morning.

The US now led 8–4. The fightback that Olazábal had desperately hoped for had not materialized. Instead, his team's predicament had got far worse. It was a commanding lead. Many were already conceding privately that it would not be overcome. The Americans had proved conclusively that they were the better team, they said. They had the better captain, they had been better prepared and they were riding the home advantage for all it was worth.

In the media marquee, the British Sunday newspaper journalists finished off their first-edition pieces. Afternoon was sliding into evening back in the UK and deadlines had to be met. Some of the pieces were not particularly complimentary about Olazábal. How could they be in the circumstances? Such are the perils of trying to write about the outcome of an event before it has finished.

Most famously, a similar scenario caught British writers out at the 1999 Champions League final between Manchester United and Bayern Munich in Barcelona. The match was played on a Wednesday night and pressure of deadlines meant that the vast majority of copy had to be filed before the final whistle.

United were heavily outplayed in the final and were 1–0 down as the match entered injury time. The pieces that had been written reflected that and many were brutal in their assessment of Sir Alex Ferguson's tactical failings on the night. Then, in the frenetic final seconds, Teddy Sheringham equalized and Ole Gunnar Solskjaer grabbed a winner for United.

It was too late to change most of the pieces for the first edition. In most cases, the first paragraph was scrapped and a replacement one hastily inserted to reflect the dramatic change in circumstances. In later editions, newspaper journalists tore up what they had written before and started again. Their pieces this time paid tribute to Ferguson and his fantastic achievement in winning the match and the Treble for United.

Not much escapes Ferguson, though. At the start of the following season, he was talking to journalists at a press conference when the subject of the Champions League final came up. He fixed one of them with an icy stare. 'I saw all the first edition pieces, you know,' he said.

Olazábal may have felt the same about what was written for the Sunday papers at Medinah but the writers really had little alternative. It was shaping up as a humiliating defeat. Everyone had expected it would be close. Some had thought the Americans might just shade it. No one had anticipated a slaughter like this.

McDowell was candid about the position Europe now found themselves in. 'We are in a hole,' he said. 'These guys, there's blood in the water and they are up for it. They have got a head of steam up and we have got to try and stop it this afternoon. It was hard out there this morning. It was very hard to ignore the red on the board. It's hard to ignore the noise that's being made around the golf course. We are trying to concentrate on our game and we are trying to get our job done. We just had two sessions in a row now where we made nothing, and consequently when that happens, you are going to lose to great teams.'

The Americans, in stark contrast, were on a high. They had taken down the world number one again and their opponents seemed utterly demoralized. In the media marquee later, Dustin Johnson talked about the crowd and how the roar he had got when he walked on to the 18th green that afternoon was the loudest he had ever heard at a golf course. 'Especially for me,' he added.

The hordes of American fans streamed towards the refreshment marquees and stocked up on beer before the afternoon fourballs session. They thought it was all over. The autumn sun was shining. The temperature was rising. They thought it was time for the victory party.

'I got the monkey off my back,' Snedeker said after McIlroy and McDowell had been vanquished. 'Losing to them yesterday was kind of hard to take, to give away that half a point on 18 the way I drove it, but when you've got a player like Jim, you're never out of it. Jim played great coming down the stretch yesterday and he played great again today. I can't tell you how much pressure there was on those shots coming down the stretch and he just flagged it right every time. It's fun to have a partner like that behind you.'

Even Furyk, the lugubrious bad-news bear of so many American Ryder Cup teams, was starting to feel good. Even Furyk, the decent guy who had got used to heartbreaking failures, was starting to acknowledge that this time it was going to be different. This time, it was going to feel sweet to rub European noses in it.

'I feel fortunate,' Furyk said, 'but we played well, and I'm proud of my partner here. He played like a champ. If there's anyone on the team now that I want standing over a five-footer that I just ran by the hole or left short, I want this guy over that five-footer, I promise you.'

As for McIlroy, the Americans thought they had him where they wanted him. They thought they were beginning to see the body language that signified he was downcast and giving up. They thought he was in the shoulder-slumping territory that

Paul Azinger had talked about earlier in the week.

'We just sort of plotted our way around the golf course,' McIlroy said disconsolately. 'We made a couple of birdies coming in but it just wasn't enough. We got behind early again and then we tried our hardest to get back into the match but we just couldn't get there.'

McDowell would not come back out in the afternoon. McIlroy would. His Ryder Cup had started slowly but it was about to take flight.

12 Dubya and a heartbeat

At the 1999 Ryder Cup at Brookline, the American captain Ben Crenshaw and the then Texas governor, George W. Bush, went into the US team room to read an address from the Battle of the Alamo. The Americans were down. They needed inspiration and Bush provided some. After he had finished reading, the normally mild-mannered David Duval rushed out, screaming: 'Let's go out and kill them.'

On Saturday afternoon at Medinah, Bush was there again. This time, things were a whole lot more relaxed. He was sitting in a cavalcade of golf buggies assembled in a patch of open space that lay between the right side of the 5th green and the 6th tee. His father, George H. W. Bush, the 41st President of the United States, was sitting in another buggy with his sprightly wife, Barbara.

Dubya was sitting with Davis Love. He was here to bestow his congratulations on the US team. That much was obvious. He was in a good spot to cheer them on their way and indulge in a bit of back-slapping. He wasn't involved in the upcoming presidential race, of course, but he liked the cameras and golf has always been his thing.

Dubya and his golf clubs had provided one of the most memorable moments in Michael Moore's 2004 documentary *Fahrenheit 9/11* about what happened to the States after the September 11 atrocities. In some news footage filmed in 2002, Bush is seen addressing reporters and talking solemnly about a spate of suicide bombings that had caused devastation in Israel.

'I call upon all nations to do everything they can to stop these terrorist killers,' Bush says to the camera. 'Thank you.'

His speech over, Bush turns away and it becomes obvious he is holding a golf club in his hand. He turns back to the camera with a smile on his face. 'Now watch this drive,' he says.

Moore used the footage as an example of Bush's shallowness and insincerity. He certainly looked like he was far more enthused about golf than matters of state. And now, as he chatted with a deferential Captain Love, it looked as if he was in a position of power again, ready to give his blessing to the American players as they marched through on their way to victory.

He had got there too late to greet the opening matches of the afternoon, Bubba Watson and Webb Simpson against Justin Rose and Francesco Molinari, and Dustin Johnson and Matt Kuchar against Nicolas Colsaerts and Paul Lawrie. But Watson and Simpson didn't need his help. They were already cruising to another crushing victory. And Johnson and Kuchar, another of Love's expertly chosen pairs, were heading for another impressive win of their own.

It was the matches that were heading his way now that ex-President George W. Bush had come to see. First of all, he wanted to see Tiger Woods, who was hoping to get his first point on the board, by partnering Steve Stricker to victory against Luke Donald and Sergio García. Bush had been a sinner himself, too, before he had turned away from alcohol. He had no problem in being seen communing with Tiger.

And following Woods was Rory McIlroy, anchoring the European team again and this time in tandem with Ian Poulter. This was probably as close as Olazábal had to a Dream Team at the Ryder Cup but it looked as though he had brought them together too late. The first two fourball matches were going America's way. They were heading for a 10–4 lead.

The US domination had got to the point now where nobody was speculating about the outcome any more. It was assumed the US had won. Conversation turned to issues like what would have happened if the Americans had won two or three more matches and achieved 14½ points for overall victory by Saturday evening. Would the players even have to come back and play the singles on Sunday? Nobody knew the answer, and anyway that was academic now. The point was that Europe's position looked utterly hopeless.

Nobody was expecting too much of Donald and García, either. Neither of them had won a point in the competition so far. Both had looked fretful and out of sorts. Donald had been on the wrong end of two heavy beatings by Phil Mickelson and Keegan Bradley, one of which he shared with Donald. They had once considered themselves a formidable partnership but their lustre had seemingly faded.

If there was any reason for optimism it was that they were playing against Woods and Stricker who had also lost their opening two games. Woods, in particular, was under pressure not to make it three on the spin and excite more vitriolic reactions about how he didn't care about the competition. He had been rested in the morning for the first time in his Ryder Cup career. He was determined to put things right.

It was shortly before 1 p.m. and the temperature had risen to 75 degrees when the players appeared on the first tee. García started fast and spun his approach shot back to within two feet of the cup. Woods' approach shot through the back of the green, Stricker's came to a halt 15 feet from the pin. Woods hit a beautiful chip to within three feet but it was not enough. When Stricker left his birdie putt short, the US conceded García's putt and Europe were 1 up.

At last, something was going Europe's way. At the 2nd, Stricker's tee-shot hit the left side of the green and bounced into the lake. Woods had to be cautious and left his tee-shot 40 feet from the hole in the rough. Donald and García were both on the green, both with makeable birdie chances. Both missed but after Woods' chip had run six feet past the hole, he still had an uncomfortable putt for par that he needed to halve the hole. He thought he had it but it veered right at the last moment, caught the lip and stayed out. Donald and García were 2 up.

Maybe Europe could at least salvage a little dignity from a terrible day. Woods seemed to be just about the only American who had not caught the good vibe. He was playing horribly. His approach at the 3rd was another shocker, flying through the back of the green. He compounded his error with his next effort, a flop shot that fell way short of the putting surface. Mickelson, watching from the gallery, would have done a lot better.

With Stricker also struggling, Europe had the chance to go 3 up. Donald faced an eight-foot putt for birdie to win the hole but he pushed it just wide of the cup. It was only a temporary reprieve for the Americans. Woods was all over the place again on the 4th, hooking his tee-shot into the rough, trying to hack out but hitting even deeper into trouble. It was up to Stricker to try to win the hole but his 10-foot putt lipped out. García was closer and he drained his. Europe were 3 up. After all the setbacks of the previous three sessions, this was unfamiliar territory for the Europeans.

The two former Presidents were waiting up ahead, though, and the Americans responded. Woods and Stricker both made it on to the green at the par-five 5th in two. Both had putts for eagle to win the hole and reduce the Europeans' advantage. Woods' effort turned right just short of the hole but Stricker nailed his effort. It brought a smile to Dubya's face.

Dubya had parked his buggy pretty much in the middle of a straight line running from the 5th green to the 6th tee so Woods had little choice but to greet him as he passed. After he teed off at the sixth, the elder George Bush asked his buggy driver to motor over a few yards to intercept the players as they headed off down the fairway. President Bush stayed seated as he chatted with Tiger. He inquired how things were going. 'I need to play better,' Woods said, showing that, if only with former Presidents, he was capable of humility. Stricker kept on walking. He seemed to realize that his presence was not required.

The 6th and 7th holes were halved but on the short 8th, Donald sparked into life. His tee-shot stopped three feet from the hole and with Woods in a greenside bunker and Stricker facing a putt of 25 feet, the European pair was in control again. Stricker missed his birdie putt by a fraction and Donald rolled his in, sending Europe 3 up once more.

At the 9th, Woods' woes continued when he missed a four-foot putt for par and Donald drained his effort from a similar distance for birdie. Europe was now 4 up but suddenly Woods began to find some form. He had played beautifully on the back nine during the defeat to Colsaerts and Westwood in the previous afternoon's fourballs and, after the turn, his play seemed to go up a gear against Donald and García, too.

At the par-five 10th, he got a piece of luck when his second shot ran through the greenside bunker and on to the putting surface. His eagle attempt stopped two feet short but it was enough. The Europeans conceded his birdie and when García missed right, the deficit was cut to three holes.

It was just the right time for Woods and Stricker to glimpse some momentum. It seemed as though huge roars for American advances were coming from all around them. Up ahead, Simpson was sinking in his fifth birdie in five holes as the US juggernaut rolled on. The crowd following that match was working itself into a frenzy of triumphal patriotism.

With Michael Jordan and Dubya looking on, Stricker got in on the act and birdied the 12th to cut the Europeans' lead to two holes. The day had gone so badly for Olazábal's team that suddenly it seemed entirely logical that Donald and García might be about to blow a four-hole lead and lose the game. Almost everything else that could have gone wrong that day had gone wrong.

Woods was in a groove now, too. On they went to the 13th, perhaps the best amphitheatre hole on the course where around 15,000 spectators gathered on the wooded hillsides that rose up from Lake Kadijah as it shielded the front of the green. Woods hit his tee-shot over the lake to within five feet. No one else got that close. When everyone had taken their tee-shot, the growing circus of journalists, teammates, wives, camera crews and officials scurried down the hill towards the wooden bridge that led to the green.

Those are the moments when the atmosphere at the Ryder Cup is unbeatable, when it feels as though fans are all around you, above you, to both sides, their yells and cheers roaring in the ears of the players. Woods marched over that bridge like a man who knew his opponents were vulnerable. 'Birdies will be like gold dust at the 13th,' García had predicted before the competition. But Woods just waited for the others to miss, then sank his birdie putt. The Europeans had lost three of the last four and were now just one hole ahead.

Woods birdied the 14th, too, but Donald stopped the US drawing all square when he holed his own birdie putt from seven feet having been in the greenside bunker. At the 15th, both Donald and Woods found sand off the tee and Donald made the better recovery. At last, Europe halted the American charge. Woods missed his shot at a third successive birdie short and right but Donald, from four feet away, made no mistake. Europe were 2 up again with three to play. They had gained some breathing space.

Woods refused to be discouraged. He had taken charge of the group now. He struck his tee-shot down the middle of the fairway at the 16th and then hit his approach to within nine feet. With García and Donald spraying their approaches left and right, the hole was within Woods' reach. He buried his birdie putt and then pointed in triumph to the hole. He was on a roll that was going to be hard to stop. Europe's advantage was reduced to one hole again.

Graeme McDowell had said earlier there was blood in the water and Woods could smell it now. After spending most of the competition cursing his inadequacies, he was in hot pursuit. He took an eight-iron for his tee-shot at the par-three 17th and stuck it to within five feet of the hole. The galleries around the green erupted. The roar was deafening. Europe's quest to retain the Ryder Cup was on the brink of total collapse.

Then came one of the most dramatic moments of the competition, a moment the Europeans would look back upon afterwards and identify as the first hazy glimpse of salvation. After García had played, Donald stepped up for his tee-shot. The American celebrations were still going on all around the green. Woods' teammates were gathered there, too, waiting to acclaim him when he strode across the bridge over Lake Kadijah. Against that backdrop, in the midst of all that hostility, surrounded by American fans raucous from drinking all afternoon, confronted by a shot over water with everything on the line, Donald stepped up and put his ball even closer to the pin than Tiger's.

'Tiger hit it close,' Donald said afterwards, 'so I thought I'd better hit it close, too. I was hoping to hole it.'

What a moment that was. The Europeans among the crowd went wild. Perhaps it would mean nothing but at least it felt like a shot of tremendous courage and considerable defiance. It was a signal that despite being assailed by so much adversity, despite wilting in the face of the American assault, Europe had not given up.

Woods made his putt for birdie. Donald had to do the same or the match would be all square going to the last and the momentum would be with the US. Donald nailed it to great cheers of rejoicing from the European contingent grouped around the hole. Europe were guaranteed half a point. They knew that wouldn't be enough.

By now, Woods and Stricker were the only Americans on the US team not to win any points. Of the 54 holes they had played on Friday and Saturday, they had held the lead for only three. So they had personal pride to play for, too. They both striped their tee-shots down the fairway at the 18th. So did García. Donald found the bunker and could get no nearer than 40 yards from the green with his second shot.

Woods was the dangerman for Europe. He had hit five

birdies on the back nine and now he was about 20 feet from the hole, eyeing another. Stricker was only eight feet away. Woods putted first and missed to the right. Donald was out of the equation. García stepped up to try to make a birdie to win the match but backed off before he putted.

The crowd loved that. They booed and jeered him. García composed himself and walked up to the ball again. He missed to the right. Now Stricker, the oldest man on either team, had a chance to rescue something from the mediocrity of his performances so far. He had an eight-foot putt to kill off the Ryder Cup to win the hole, halve the match and kill off the Ryder Cup. He pushed it left. It hit the lip and rolled on.

'We fought hard,' Woods said, painfully aware he had still won nothing for his team. 'Unfortunately, it just wasn't enough. We gave ourselves two good looks at eighteen and didn't get it done.'

It was the fourth time García had beaten Woods in a Ryder Cup match, having suffered only one defeat, and it was the first point for either García or Donald in the competition. But it was about much more than that. The European victory breathed some life back into the Ryder Cup. Only a little but enough to bring Olazábal some cheer.

'We wanted it because we knew it was very important to the team,' a grinning García said afterwards. 'We were trying very hard. The way Luke played coming in was amazing. The way he held the match together on the back nine was amazing. I was struggling a little bit this week. I didn't feel very comfortable, but I putted well, I hit some good birdies and then he took over.'

Donald is not the type to show much emotion. When he does, he usually looks embarrassed a split second later. But when he got back to the Media Centre after the match, it was obvious he was elated. He had given his team a little hope and in the process he had given his confidence a huge boost for the task that lay ahead on Sunday.

'We knew it was going to be a tough match this afternoon,' he said. 'You never give up against Tiger and Stricker. They are a formidable pairing and they played great on the back nine. They birdied all the tough holes like twelve and thirteen, Tiger hit an unbelievable shot there and again on sixteen. The holes where you thought par may have been good enough for a half, you needed birdie.

'I felt really calm all day. I don't know why but I just did. They played great coming down the back stretch. They were making birdies all the time and I knew we had to do the same. We had to hold them off. We hung in there and we were able to match birdies on seventeen, which was key for us, and we just held on there right at the last. That was big. It has a given us a lift that we needed. It's given us a heartbeat for tomorrow.'

A heartbeat. Just a faint one. But McIlroy and Poulter were still out on the course. The heartbeat was about to get stronger.

13 Poulter, the defiant one

This was the dream for Ian Poulter. This was how to live it. The last game out on Saturday afternoon and 40,000 people out on the course. Most of them American. Most of them tanked up. Most of them cheering and roaring until they were hoarse. All of them desperate for Poulter to lose. All of them thinking the Ryder Cup was already won.

It felt like playing in front of an English football crowd out there, something that Poulter had always wanted to do. It felt raw and loud and maybe even a little unsafe and unboundaried. It felt like the gloves were off. It felt like everything, absolutely everything, was on the line.

What else made it a dream? This. Poulter was out there with the world number one. He was out there with Rory McIlroy, the kid everybody said was the new Tiger Woods, the kid everybody said would be the world number one for a long time, the kid with the ridiculous talent, the wunderkind, golf's new superstar.

But nobody was looking at McIlroy. Everybody was looking at Poulter. Nobody had McIlroy down as the leader of this pair.

When everything was on the line, when it was win or bust, everybody's eyes were on Poulter. Everybody put their faith in him. Everybody willed him on. Everybody got behind him. Him. Rory, too. But mostly him. In a way, this was what he had dreamed of all those years ago when he gave that interview to *Golf World*. This was his Just Me and Tiger moment. No one was laughing about that quote now, were they? Not this weekend. This was him out there with the new world number one and everyone thinking he, Ian Poulter, was the better player.

This was him saying to himself that he was going to take charge of this match. That he was going to win this match. That he was going to drag Europe back into a Ryder Cup that everybody thought had finished some time around Saturday lunchtime. This was him saying that right here, right now, in Medinah on the last weekend of September 2012, Ian Poulter was the best player in the world.

The best player, the player no one could touch, the player no one could live with, the player that unnerved the others with the intensity of his play, who got so carried away with what he was trying to do that it looked as if his eyes were going to pop right out of his head. This was his moment. He knew it was. He knew he was going to seize it.

He knew it would not be easy. In fact, he knew it would be hellishly hard. He had to get himself up again for a start. Had to raise himself back up to the emotional pitch he had reached for the other two games he had been involved with, partnering his mate Justin Rose. He had managed the Herculean task of taking down Bubba Watson and Webb Simpson in the morning. No one else got close to doing that. The other two matches they played, Watson and Simpson won 5&4. Now Poulter had to start again.

Now he and McIlroy were up against another unbeaten American pair. Jason Dufner and Zach Johnson were probably the partnership with the lowest profile on the US team but they had been getting the job done. They had beaten Lee Westwood and Francesco Molinari in the Friday morning foursomes and Nicolas Colsaerts and Sergio García in the Saturday morning foursomes. They did their job calmly and efficiently. They were fine players.

They were dangerous opponents for Poulter, too. Because they were quieter, low-key, they didn't provide quite the same instant motivation as playing against an extrovert like Watson or his old enemy Woods. Poulter tried to remind himself of that on the tee. They were top, top players. He would need to be at his Ryder Cup best, inspired and half-crazed, to win this.

Maybe that was why he started slowly. Because it wasn't Woods. Because it wasn't Bubba with his pink driver and his exhortations to the crowd. Whatever, Johnson birdied the first and put the US 1 up. On the 2nd, Poulter only just cleared the water. McIlroy didn't even manage that. His ball was in Lake Kadijah. Poulter chipped to within six feet, but missed his putt for par. Dufner and Johnson were now 2 up.

This was not the way it was supposed to be. This was not the role Poulter had been envisaging. That's the problem when you are supposed to be the heart and soul of a team. A thorough beating is not permitted, particularly if it means the loss of the point that finally extinguishes all hope.

That would be the kind of result that would not fit particularly well on Poulter's CV. It would be a stain on his Ryder Cup record. It would damage the aura that had built up around him in the competition. It would be hard for him to deal with. It would make his failures in Majors harder to deal with, not easier. It would take away his consolation.

Poulter missed the green with his approach to the 3rd. He relied on McIlroy to halve the hole. Still 2 down. Then, at the 4th, Poulter sparked into life. Johnson and Dufner missed birdie putts and now Poulter had a chance from 15 feet. He sank the putt and let out a great roar of triumph and relief. The first of the afternoon and not the last.

Poulter and McIlroy both birdied the 5th. They thought they had won the hole. Then Dufner sank a 40-footer. Hole halved. Poulter and McIlroy were both in the bunker at the 6th. Both saved par. Another hole halved. Poulter and McIlroy both missed makeable putts for birdie at the 7th. Dufner made his makeable putt. The Americans were up by two again.

The 8th was halved as was the 9th. The Americans seemed to be consolidating their lead. McIlroy was struggling to get anything going again. Poulter was searching for the devil inside. Poulter and Johnson both sank long birdie putts at the 10th to halve the hole. The 11th was halved. Johnson's tee-shot at the next crashed into an oak tree. Dufner drove into the rough. Both recovered. The 12th was halved. It was a war of attrition. It seemed like the Americans would never crack.

Then everything changed. Poulter found the bunker from the 13th tee. McIlroy didn't. His tee-shot sailed over the waters of Lake Kadijah and landed eight feet from the hole. Dufner had a good chance for birdie, too, but missed it. McIlroy's putt, though, was dead centre. The Europeans had won the hole. They had broken the stalemate. They had smashed a hole in the wall and now they rushed through.

McIlroy's birdie unleashed something in Poulter. Maybe it was that he didn't want to play a supporting role to anyone. He hadn't done so far in this Ryder Cup. Why should he start now? Or maybe it was the fact that McIlroy was rising to the challenge, too, that inspired him. Maybe he took strength from the fact that McIlroy was fighting just as hard for the team.

Because what is beyond doubt in everything that has been written and said about Poulter and the Ryder Cup is that he loves the team. He draws strength from the team. He provides them with inspiration, sure, but he draws inspiration from them, too. He drew inspiration from them all weekend. From Olazábal, from Rose, from the spirit of Ballesteros, and now from McIlroy.

Poulter was candid about that later. He is stronger in a group than he is on his own. Sometimes he needs someone to chide him or to encourage him. Sometimes he needed to be jolted out of a bad rhythm. Sometimes he needs support. And when he gets it, he can be capable of some of the most sublime and irresistible golf anybody has ever seen.

That was how he began to play now. A few minutes after the round finished, Dufner summed up the helplessness of his situation, the sheer impotence that can hobble you when you are playing Poulter in the Ryder Cup. 'It stinks to lose,' Dufner said, 'but you have to tip your cap when you run into a buzzsaw like that.'

A buzzsaw. Exactly. For the last six holes, that is exactly what Poulter was. An instrument made of steel that cut through everything in its way. Nothing could stop him. For everything that happened on Sunday, those six holes were probably the most important holes of the 39th Ryder Cup. They changed everything. Poulter changed everything.

Poulter needed to birdie the 14th to stop the Americans taking a two-hole lead again. He did it, getting up and down from the front bunker. At the 15th, he again found the bunker. It looked like he was in trouble. But he played a stunning shot out of the sand to within a foot of the hole. Johnson was suddenly flustered. He had hit his drive into the water. Poulter was so close to the cup, the Americans conceded his birdie. Now, for the first time, the Europeans were level. The match was all square.

At the 16th, McIlroy missed a four-foot putt for par. Poulter had a fiendish, slaloming 15-foot putt for birdie. He made it. Dufner needed to hole a 10-footer to halve the hole. He missed it. Poulter and McIlroy were 1 up with two to play, ahead for the first time in the match. It was a breathtaking turnaround but there was plenty more to come.

At the next, McIlroy was off the 17th green. He was a bystander by now and he knew it. Poulter was playing like he was in a trance. He hit a pinpoint tee-shot to eight feet. Johnson played next and bettered it. He was inside Poulter. He had a shorter putt for birdie. Poulter knew he probably had to make the putt if Europe were to stay ahead. He made the putt. Johnson made his putt, too, just like Poulter knew he would. Europe were 1 up with one to play.

The sun was starting to set. Things were getting a little rowdy by the 18th green. Some of the European fans were encouraged by this late rally but the Americans thought they knew better. They baited them about the hopelessness of their situation. They taunted them and said this was way too little, way too late. They said it was still over. There was a bit of finger-jabbing, a few drunken insults. Nothing worse than that.

Poulter played first. He found the middle of the fairway. His approach landed flush on the green but there was one last obstacle to overcome. Dufner was on the green, too, and his approach had come to rest three feet from the hole. It was a staggering shot. He rolled his putt in for a simple birdie. McIlroy missed, so it was down to Poulter. Again.

It was a difficult putt. He was 15 feet away. The read was

right to left. The speed was not an issue. It was downhill. Poulter knew he couldn't miss. He had shot four straight birdies already. One more wasn't going to be a big deal. Not when he was feeling like this. He thought about his team. He thought about not letting them down. Poulter stood over it and struck it. It rolled and then it disappeared. Poulter had done it. 'Come on,' he yelled, his eyes bulging, his chest puffed out. 'Come on.' McIlroy looked at him in awe.

The American fans around the green melted away. It was a strange end to their day. Their team had dominated it. They still felt like celebrating. They still thought Sunday was going to be a party. But there was a little doubt in their minds now. Just a nagging concern. There was still some life left in the Europeans. They knew that now.

The European fans stayed on. They celebrated as if they had won the Ryder Cup. It was nearly dark by then. Some of the players went over to the ropes to have their picture taken with knots of happy supporters and to chat with friends. The mood was different. It had lifted. Camera flashes illuminated the green and turned dusk into daylight. It didn't feel like a humiliation any more. It felt like there was going to be a fight.

Olazábal was filled with a mixture of relief and exhilaration. But overriding all that, he was filled with a deep sense of gratitude towards Poulter. Olazábal understood the role he had played. He understood the debt he and the team owed him. He understood that by himself, Poulter was responsible for half of Europe's points at that stage. And he understood, too, that in Poulter he could see some of the guts, the fight and the passion he had once seen in Ballesteros.

'I think the Ryder Cup should build a statue to him,' Olazábal said. 'That's Poulter. That's why we say he's such a special character for this event. He thrives at this event. He loves to be in the spotlight. He loves to be in the kind of situations that he found himself in just now coming down the back nine. And what he did today was just outstanding, period.'

There were times towards the end of the round when McIlroy had seemed almost unnerved by Poulter. He had looked at him as if he did not quite understand what was happening. He was seeing a transformation in a man. He was seeing a spirit gripping him but he could not quite understand how it worked. He had seemed a little like a startled bystander watching Dr Bruce Banner turning into the Incredible Hulk.

'It's intense,' McIlroy said. 'It's very intense. I don't know, he just gets that look in his eye, especially when he makes one of those big putts, and he's fist-pumping, and he'll just look right through you. When Poults gets that look in his eye the week of the Ryder Cup, it's very impressive. It's great to see, great to see the enthusiasm and the passion that he has for this event, like all of us do. But this event definitely brings the best out of Ian, and I'm glad it did today.

'If it wasn't for him, we wouldn't be in this position. We would have a much, much tougher task tomorrow to try to make up the points. We just needed something to get going today. We were a little flat out there playing at the back of the pack. We had a couple of good chances on eleven, didn't go in. We had a good chance on twelve. And then I think getting that birdie on thirteen really gave us the little bit of momentum, the spark that we needed. I could have just walked into the clubhouse at that point. I wasn't really needed after that. Ian sort of took over. It was the Poults show from there on in, and it was just a joy to watch. All the credit needs to be put on this man.'

And Poulter? He sat back and lapped it up. This was his moment, he knew that. He was the leader again. Whatever happened now, that would not change. He was the one who had stood up when someone had to. He was the one who had stood firm against the Americans when the rest seemed to be falling away. Sitting there on the dais at the Media Centre, it must have felt as good to him as if he had just won a Major.

'If there was a world ranking system solely for match play,' Poulter was asked, 'where would you rank yourself?'

'Zero,' Poulter said.

Sitting next to him, Sergio García smiled mischievously.

'That's better than one,' García said.

'I surprise myself sometimes,' Poulter said, grinning. 'Match play; I love the fight of it. I mean, you get to stare your opponent straight in the face, and sometimes that's what you need to do. The Ryder Cup means an awful lot to every one of us. There's a lot of passion in that team room and there are reasons why we want to keep that trophy as long as possible. This event is just so big to every one of us, and we love it. I love it.

'It comes from within. And you know, if we can do anything to get this trophy in this position, and Seve is looking down on us, then you've got to do what you've got to do. We knew we had to get back at them this afternoon. We knew we had to make birdies and, wow, five in a row. It was awesome. I've got the world number one by my side backing me up and it allows me to go ahead and hit some golf shots. You know what, it's pretty fun, this Ryder Cup.

'After the thirteenth, my putter warmed up nicely then it just went crazy. It was tough out there for the Europeans today. We're in Chicago, they've had a few drinks today and they weren't making it easy for us. I will be honest, it was brutal.'

Their opponents were gracious to the last. They felt they could afford to be. And Zach Johnson's warm praise after the match came with a kicker. 'They birdied the last six holes and

Poulter birdied the last five holes by himself,' Johnson said. 'It wasn't like we gave it to them, either. We had opportunities. We missed a couple of putts but made some putts, too. That was just a buzzsaw at the end. There's nothing you can do, just tip your hat and shake his hand. The beauty of where we're at is we are up 10–6, I guess.'

That's what all the Americans guessed. They still had a handsome lead. They were still on a high from everything that had happened. They had taken note of Poulter's achievements but they told themselves he could only win one point the next day. It was out of his hands.

The Europeans were beginning to feel differently. McIlroy spoke with great perspicacity. He pointed out that the American partnerships had bonded particularly well and they had drawn great strength from playing with each other. 'It's going to be weird for them getting split up,' McIlroy pointed out.

One man, of course, was more bullish than the rest. Ian Poulter was already thinking about making history, about doing what the Americans had done at Brookline in 1999, about shocking the golfing world. 'That point in the last match is huge for the team,' Poulter said. 'It's given the whole team a massive boost, to be able to go into tomorrow knowing that you can win from this position.'

Poulter swallowed hard and made another guarantee. 'It's been done in the past,' he said. 'It's going to be done again.'

14 #whatwouldsevedo?

Most people still thought it was over. The idea of a European comeback was just a fantasy. It had been a great summer for British sport. Probably the best ever. But it was fanciful to think it could end with a miracle. Sure, the Americans had done it at Brookline but they were at home then. Europe were the away team this time. The galleries would not be roaring them on come Sunday. They would be in party mood, urging their team over the line so they could begin the celebrations in earnest.

The US team was not shaken by Poulter's heroics. They viewed it as an admirable cameo. Nothing more. It was too little, too late, as far as they were concerned. Davis Love III was desperate to guard against complacency but others had already relaxed because they thought the job was done. The task facing Europe, Gene Wojciechowski wrote on ESPN.com, was 'as close to insurmountable as trying to climb Mt. Everest wearing a T-shirt, cargo shorts and flip-flops'.

Wojciechowski did not go in for half measures when he sat down at his computer on Saturday night. He lampooned the European team mercilessly. So mercilessly that his article was reprinted in some English papers on Tuesday morning just for the fun of it. Nevertheless, his merry-making was symptomatic of the general air of jubilation around the American camp at the end of the second day's play.

'For those who think this Ryder Cup is finished, think again,' Wojciechowski wrote. 'Team Europe can still win if the following things happen Sunday. One: Keegan Bradley is abducted. Two: Team USA captain Davis Love III inserts Cup spectators Michael Jordan, President George W. Bush, Amy Mickelson and the Rev. Jesse Jackson into the singles lineup.' And so it went on; all very droll. But all very forgivable, too. If the roles had been reversed, European journalists would have been enjoying themselves immensely at the Americans' expense. English readers would have woken up to gleeful headlines about the Massacre of Medinah on Sunday morning and the Americans would have been lambasted for their ineptitude.

Love was not complacent but he was confident. He had every right to be. The American team room was a happy place on Saturday night. President George Bush Sr and President George Bush Jr had both dropped in and Love had spoken on the telephone to President Clinton, who had been present at the American defeat at the K Club outside Dublin in 2006. Love described it as 'a keep-up-the-good-work call'.

Everybody expected that the veterans in the American side would counsel strongly against believing that the Cup was already won. They would remind their less experienced colleagues about what had happened at Brookline, surely. They would say that they needed to keep their foot on Europe's throat and stop them gaining any sort of momentum on Sunday morning. 'Things were going according to plan,' Love wrote later. 'In Session IV, Europe, and most especially Ian Poulter, caught fire late and won two matches. Still, everything was good.'

At Celtic Manor, the US had won six and halved two of the twelve singles matches; at Valhalla, they had won seven and halved one. The singles were supposed to be their forte. It was in that format where the camaraderie the Europeans had come to draw upon was negated and that the superior rankings of the Americans were finally supposed to be borne out. So, if anything, most expected that the US would extend their lead on Sunday and turn their dominance of the first two days into a rout.

So Love could warn against complacency as much as he wanted but most were convinced the Sunday singles were little more than a formality. 'Team USA needs to win 4 and a half points,' Wojciechowski wrote in his ill-starred Saturday night piece. 'That's not a gimme putt, but it's almost within the circle of friendship.'

It was also pointed out that four of the men Europe would have to count on if any fightback was to take shape had not yet won a point. Peter Hanson, Paul Lawrie, Francesco Molinari and Martin Kaymer had all looked dreadfully out of sorts so far. Hanson and Kaymer had not been trusted to hit a ball in either of Saturday's sessions. Even if Europe got off to a flier, sooner or later the Americans would get through to their tail and all would be lost. The Europeans, the US felt, had got too much to do with too little.

There was no suggestion that the European team was falling apart and no one openly criticized their levels of commitment. Quite rightly, many pointed out that the European team simply weren't making enough putts. But more and more questions were being asked about Olazábal's perceived lack of leadership. Colin Montgomerie, who seemed to be enjoying Europe's struggle just a little too much, said that the team was now in 'crisis'.

There was widespread criticism of Olazábal's decision to rest Poulter on Friday afternoon and to persevere with Lee

Westwood on Saturday morning when his form had been so shaky. Most of all, there was bafflement at Olazábal's captaincy style. He had been so low-key it was almost unnerving. There was a feeling that the team needed inspirational leadership to rally it and that Olazábal was probably incapable of providing it.

And the kind of commanding lead that the US held brought with it certain dangers. A narrow lead keeps players taut and tense and on their game. A healthy lead can make them relax. It happens in other sports, too. In tennis, when one man wins the first two sets and the other wins the next three. In football, too. The most famous example, perhaps, was the 2005 Champions League final in Istanbul when Liverpool went back to their changing room at half-time 3–0 down having been completely outplayed for 45 minutes by AC Milan.

Steven Gerrard, the Liverpool captain, said after the match that as he was walking off, he was clinging to the hope that perhaps two of the Milan players had gone to their dressing room believing that the match was over and they could switch off. That was all it took, Gerrard said. If two players relaxed and let their concentration slip, there was a way back. And so it turned out. Liverpool scored three goals in six minutes in the second half and won the trophy after a penalty shoot-out.

There was not a flicker of a thought in the US team room, as they mingled with their ex-presidents and mulled over what had already been achieved, that the tide would turn the next day. But the mood among the European players had finally lifted. There was nothing left to lose any more. Poulter's string of five birdies and his clutch putt on the 18th were most responsible for that but another dynamic was developing, too.

Later on Saturday evening, Graeme McDowell sent out a tweet with the hashtag '#whatwouldsevedo?'. It was clear that the team were trying to draw on Ballesteros for inspiration and that they had begun to believe something special was possible. Olazábal might have appeared to be lacking in passion for most of the competition but now he stepped things up a gear.

On Friday night, Olazábal had been angry with his players at the end of the day. 'We got the hair dryer treatment,' McDowell said about the angry note Olazábal had struck at the end of the first day's play. McIlroy corroborated him. 'We got a roasting from him,' the world number one said. 'It was real Sir Alex Ferguson stuff.'

But now it was different. Olazábal made a passionate speech about what the Ryder Cup meant to him and how he believed in each and every one of his 12 players. He believed each of them was capable of winning their match the next day. He said his faith in them had not been shaken.

And he spoke about Ballesteros, too. He spoke about what Ballesteros would do in this situation with his back against the wall. He told his team that Seve would have come out fighting, that he would have struggled to the last. Several of the European players were in tears.

Different players reacted to the new surge of hope in different ways. Justin Rose went back to the hotel where the players were staying, 20 minutes away from the course, and worked on his game. 'I did a lot of thinking,' Rose said. 'I took my clubs back to the hotel. I went back to my room and hit a few putts on the carpet. I thought, "If I'm going to win my game tomorrow, I need to do something different." For five minutes on the carpet, I clicked on to something about my grip pressure that allowed the putter to swing a little bit more freely. Just those little things; you never know when they're going to pay off.'

Luke Donald felt the change, too. He had had an uneven competition and had felt so much in need of reassurance that, with the encouragement of Olazábal and his assistants, he had been allowed to go back to his house 25 miles from Medinah for a few hours to regroup in familiar surroundings.

'Spirits were low midway through the afternoon,' Donald said, 'but when we came and won those last two matches, we really had a pep in our step. I think we just talked about it; that we still had a great chance; that we had an opportunity to make history; that Seve was watching down on us, and we hoped some of Seve's magic can rub off on the boys coming home.'

They knew by now that they had to do what had never been done before if they were to retain the Ryder Cup. They had to do what the Americans had done at Brookline in terms of overcoming a 10–6 deficit going into the final day, but they had to go one better than that because they had to do it in front of hostile crowds.

But the idea that they had to do justice to the memory of Ballesteros seemed to have grown stronger on Saturday night. All the team felt it. They would not be the first team inspired by a dead hero or a fallen teammate or a loved one who has passed away. The Manchester United team that in 1968 became the first English side to win the European Cup played with a desperation to honour the memory of former teammates who had perished in the Munich Air Disaster 10 years earlier.

At Medinah, Olazábal had done his utmost to turn the competition into a three-day tribute to Ballesteros. It was a dance with the supernatural, a hunt for the spirit of a dead hero. At times, Olazábal gave the impression that he had been conducting a séance more than giving a team talk. That afternoon, Irish bookmaker Paddy Power had used its stunt planes to post a sky tweet in the clear blue air that read 'Do it for Seve'. That was literally a message from above but on Saturday night, Olazábal seemed to have managed to breathe the fighting spirit of Ballesteros into his men.

Poulter played his part in that, too. There is no doubt that the rest of the European team were moved by Poulter's incredible show of defiance at dusk on Saturday evening. He, more than anyone else, had channelled the spirit of Ballesteros and lit the path for the rest to follow.

'The team spirit in that room on Saturday night was special,' Poulter said. 'I spoke to a few guys. We were four points behind but there was something in that team room that just sparked the whole thing. There was a glimmer of hope, something made us think we had a chance. No one really made a speech. We discussed certain things about the golf course, decisions to make on certain holes, the par fives and other bits.

'We had the pin locations, we discussed certain holes that could be key during the round. But, honestly, the team was pumped. We were really, really up. We were four points behind but it was as if we were just going out to play all square. We were ready. Did we honestly think we could win eight and a half points? Yes, we did.'

Back at the hotel, McIlroy was also feeling optimistic about Sunday. He had caught the good vibe in the European team room but he was also basing his cautious optimism on a theory he had developed about the American team. He had begun to wonder whether the tight pairings that Love had made such a virtue out of might put the Americans at a disadvantage on Sunday.

Love had not copied the famous pod system that Paul Azinger used to such great effect at Valhalla. The 2008 American captain had created three distinct four-man groups from his 12-

man roster. And the result was a shared sense that everybody had at least three guys that had their backs at all times.

There was the 'aggressive' pod of Phil Mickelson, Anthony Kim, Justin Leonard and Hunter Mahan. There was the 'steady/ supportive' pod of Stewart Cink, Chad Campbell, Ben Curtis and Steve Stricker. And there was the 'encouraging' pod of Kenny Perry, Boo Weekley, J. B. Holmes and Jim Furyk.

Love's system was more informal. He had wanted to create an 'all together now' feel in the US team, summed up by the team meal on the eve of play at which everyone – players, wives, assistants – sat at one big table.

But the American partnerships that were formed out on the course in the first two days were so tight that McIlroy wondered how the players would fare when they were separated. His hunch was that they might miss the support they had received from one another and feel exposed if Europe were able to start putting blue on the scoreboard from the start.

Jason Dufner and Zach Johnson had played with each other three times in the four sessions. So had Keegan Bradley and Phil Mickelson. So had Bubba Watson and Webb Simpson, two born-again Christians. So had Steve Stricker and Tiger Woods. Jim Furyk and Brandt Snedeker only played twice in the first four sessions but had played with each other in both matches.

In the course of those sessions, the Americans had got the kind of bond going that was usually the preserve of European Ryder Cup teams. They had drawn on team spirit and camara-derie to make them much more than the sum of their parts. They had taken energy from each other and prospered. They had developed partnerships with each other that made them feel as if they were invincible.

That was obvious in some of the margins of victory they had recorded. They got on a roll and urged each other on and on. So Mickelson and Bradley routed Luke Donald and Sergio García 4&3 in the Friday morning foursomes and Watson and Simpson trounced Paul Lawrie and Peter Hanson 5&4 in the Friday afternoon fourballs. Mickelson and Bradley were rampant on Saturday morning, too, sweeping aside Donald and Lee Westwood 7&6. And on Saturday afternoon, Watson and Simpson went into action again, thrashing Justin Rose and Francesco Molinari 5&4.

Together, Mickelson and Bradley and Watson and Simpson were formidable. Apart, McIlroy suspected, they might be a different proposition. For once, he felt the Europeans were far less reliant on each other than the Americans were. The home team had ridden the first two days on a wave of emotion and patriotism and brotherly love and it had worked beautifully for them but now they were going to have to go out and do it on their own.

Now they were going to have to go out and do it against a team that suddenly felt it had nothing to lose, a team that was drawing heavily on the kind of inspirational figure that two days of poor play could not harm. Both Olazábal and McIlroy were confident that, mentally, the Europeans were stronger than their opponents individually.

When McIlroy saw the singles draw, he was delighted that he was going up against Bradley. He relished the challenge of taking down the player who had become the on-course leader of the US team. And he knew that Bradley, playing in his first Ryder Cup and tired from the frenetic efforts of the first two days, might be vulnerable.

Donald was also delighted when he saw the draw. He was flattered that Olazábal had had enough confidence in him to put him at the head of the order even though he had had an indifferent couple of days. He was going up against

Watson, the human dynamo, who had roared around Medinah like a whirlwind.

One-on-one, Donald was confident he could neutralize Watson's verve and deprive the US of some of its emotional energy.

Poulter would be up against Simpson in the second singles group and there was a feeling that the US Open champion, another rookie, might be susceptible to pressure without Watson by his side. Poulter, of course, was Europe's superman. He was not susceptible to anything.

And then there was Rose, going up against the last of the leading American quartet, Mickelson. Rose had played poorly in the Saturday afternoon foursomes but felt more optimistic about his game after the putting session in his hotel room that evening. He, too, was determined to step up. He, too, felt the influence of Ballesteros keenly.

'This has given us a heartbeat,' Poulter said on Saturday evening after he and McIlroy had pulled off their improbable, game-changing victory over Dufner and Zach Johnson. He was even confident enough to guarantee a European victory, although no one really took much notice at the time.

As they prepared for one of the biggest days of their golfing lives, the Europeans felt they had a 13th man with them. They would be wearing his favourite final-day outfit and his image would accompany them on their rounds that day. When Love came to write about the pivotal events of the Ryder Cup in the hours after it had ended, he summed up what had happened between Saturday night and Sunday morning in two words: Enter Seve.

15

Central Time

A small crowd had gathered outside the Westin Lombard hotel in Yorktown, in the western suburbs of Chicago. From behind a police cordon, they had been watching Europe's players leaving the hotel lobby, filming on camcorders, shouting for autographs or a photograph as the golfers climbed into their courtesy cars and headed to Medinah for one of the biggest days of their sporting lives.

The players went one by one, rather than in groups or all together in a mini bus, and by 10.45 a.m. a few fans had begun to drift away. The first match in the singles, Bubba Watson v Luke Donald, began at 11.03 a.m. The rest followed at eleven-minute intervals. It stood to reason that by now, all the players were either on the way to the course or already there.

Some fans, though, were convinced that Rory McIlroy had yet to leave. They would have noticed, they said. He was the world's best golfer, one of the main reasons they had come to ogle the players as they departed. They were sure he was still inside somewhere.

Maggie Budzar, who was manning the transportation desk for the PGA of America, told some of them he had left by another exit but she could see that McIlroy's name had not been crossed off her list. It was the only one. She felt a quick surge of concern. She phoned the course to check that he had not left without telling her but was told he was not there. So she phoned the European Tour at Medinah. She might as well have rung a giant alarm bell.

McIlroy was still at the hotel. He had a room on the 14th floor of the Westin and he had spent most of the morning in it. He had woken at 9 a.m. and telephoned his girlfriend, the former world number one tennis player Caroline Wozniacki, who was in Beijing preparing for a first round match in the China Open. Then he had been for a stroll around the hotel.

He had been watching the Golf Channel the night before and had noticed that they recorded the tee-off time for his singles match against Keegan Bradley as 12.25 p.m. He didn't realize that, as is the practice with most American newspapers, there is a general rule for kick-offs, first pitches, tip-offs and first shots in golf tournaments. It's a rule usually accompanied by an asterisk: All Times Eastern.

So even though his tee-off time might have been 12.25 p.m. for people glued to their television sets on the east coast of America, the tournament wasn't being played on the east coast. Medinah is in the Midwest. From the eastern border of Illinois thousands of miles to the west to Nebraska and Kansas, America exists on Central Time, one hour behind Eastern Time. McIlroy didn't know it yet but he was desperately late.

He sauntered round the lobby, past the steakhouse named after the late Chicago White Sox and Chicago Cubs broadcaster Harry Caray. He went back to his room. He saw a couple of calls flash up on his phone, early inquiries about his whereabouts from some of the army of back-up staff with the European team, but he did not recognize the numbers, so he ignored them. Housekeeping staff were sent to his room to see if it was empty. When they knocked on his door, he sent them away without opening it.

At 11 a.m., he saw the number of his manager, Conor Ridge, on his phone. He pressed the green button. Their conversation was tense. McIlroy recounted it himself later.

'Are you at the course?' Ridge asked as soon as McIlroy picked up.

'No, I'm not,' McIlroy said.

'You're teeing off in twenty-five minutes.'

'No, I'm not, it's an hour and twenty-five.'

'You're taking the piss, you're at the golf course.'

'No, I'm not.'

'Rory, listen to me, you need to get there.'

It was then that McIlroy realized his error and a cold dread settled over him. It remains a curious oversight even given the time that has passed. McIlroy spends more and more time in the US and is selling his house on the outskirts of Belfast, intending to join the colony of European golfers already living in the States. He might only be 23 but he is hardly an innocent abroad. He's a bright man, too, sharp and down to earth. He understands the rhythms of the country well enough to know it has different time zones.

And it still beggars belief that with a huge European team support network and talk of extensive planning that left nothing to chance, there should be no safety net to catch an oversight like the one McIlroy fell prey to. This was the world's number one golfer at the start of one of the most dramatic days of the sporting year.

It would never have happened in a true team sport like cricket or football. The players would have left together in the morning. Those in charge of them would have made sure they were at the venue at least 90 minutes before the competition started. Nothing would have been left to chance. In football, in particular, the players are treated like juveniles. They are trusted with very little when it comes to their travel plans. It is assumed that leaving them to their own devices is a recipe for disaster.

Golf is different. It is an overwhelmingly individual sport. The players exist in their own small support cells. They are used to their own routines. They are used to arriving at the course alone and leaving alone. They do their own thing. Some like to arrive early to practise. Others prefer to have only a brief warm-up. McIlroy, for instance, prefers a relatively short warm-up at the course whereas a player like Padraig Harrington, fastidious and meticulous, often practises for up to two hours before he tees off. It all added up to a scenario that allowed McIlroy to fall through the net until it was almost too late.

After he took Ridge's call, McIlroy began to panic. He rushed down to the lobby and found Budzar. He was offered the SUV courtesy car that was still waiting for him or an unmarked police car. It was 12 miles to the course, a 20-minute journey with no traffic. But this was the last day of the Ryder Cup. The roads would be clogged. McIlroy chose the unmarked police car.

It was a Ford Crown Victoria, the model that author Lee Child refers to constantly in his page-turning Jack Reacher novels. Now, the Crown Vic was about to star in another thriller. McIlroy was still panicking. 'It would have been bad enough missing my tee-time playing for myself but letting down all my teammates and the whole of Europe?' he said. 'I've never been so worried in my whole life. I didn't know if I was going to make it.'

Budzar had offered to drive McIlroy to the course herself. She was acutely aware of the consequences of McIlroy being late and she did not want to entrust him to a driver who might not know the way. But she also knew a police vehicle offered

McIlroy the best chance of making it in time. She walked with him to the Crown Vic. 'There was a sense of panic by then,' she said. 'He was on the phone saying to someone he thought his tee time was 12.25. He was walking really fast.'

Lombard Deputy Police Chief Patrick Rollins had already realized there might be a problem. He had been involved in the increasingly frantic efforts to establish McIlroy's whereabouts and now it fell to him to try to get the world number one to Medinah in time. If he arrived even a minute after 11.25 a.m., he would forfeit the first hole. If he was more than five minutes late, he would forfeit the match.

Golf is steadfastly masochistic and relentlessly rigid in its adherence to the letter of the law. There is a military stiffness about it that does not allow for interpretations or grey areas. If McIlroy was late because of an oversight like this, there would have been absolutely no question of his match with Bradley being slotted in lower down the order. In golf, it is one strike and you're out.

In 2005 the South African player Retief Goosen, who was then ranked number five in the world, went to an event laid on by his new sponsor, Grey Goose vodka, the evening before the pro-am tournament that preceded the Nissan Open at the Riviera Club in Los Angeles. Goosen doesn't usually drink vodka but he had a couple that night.

He was due to tee-off in the pro-am at 6.40 a.m. the next day. He didn't make it. He was half an hour late. There was no leeway. He was disqualified from the pro-am and disqualified from the Nissan Open as well. He accepted his fate without argument. In golf, you do not have a choice. It is black and white. Rules are rules.

McIlroy knew the stakes were high. He knew instantly that if he missed his tee time, it was something that would stay with him for the rest of his career, however glorious it may turn out to be. He knew that forfeiting his match and all the accompanying upset and controversy would sabotage what slim chance his team had of dragging themselves back into the competition.

He knew that Olazábal would pay a heavy price, too, that his captaincy would be called a joke, that the organization of the European team would be derided as shambolic, that his timekeeping error would come to be seen as the symbol of a Ryder Cup many were already convinced was heading towards a heavy defeat for Europe.

So when Rollins jumped into the driver's seat, McIlroy pleaded with him to do everything he could to make the journey as fast as possible. Rollins looked across at him. 'He looked stunned and anxious,' he said. 'It looked like a lot was going through his mind. So I asked him if he'd be okay with me driving fast because of the possibility of motion sickness.'

'Just get me there,' McIlroy said. 'Get me there.'

Rollins, FBI-trained and, by his own admission, a rather poor amateur golfer, fixed emergency lights to his roof and set off on the Yorktown Mall Drive. A couple of minutes later, he was on the ramp taking him and McIlroy and the Crown Vic on to Interstate 355, heading due north towards Bloomingdale, the Chicago suburb where Medinah nestles.

Rollins radioed ahead to police at the US20 exit up ahead and told them to try to clear a path for the Crown Vic. McIlroy was a nervous wreck. 'I always knew we would make it, though he wasn't so sure,' Rollins said. 'I kept telling him we would be fine.'

By now, Olazábal and the European team were aware of the drama, too. When the alarm had first been raised by Budzar and Rollins and the rest of those involved in trying to locate McIlroy at the Westin Lombard, Olazábal had conducted an impromptu head count at the course. It confirmed McIlroy's absence.

'Everyone was asking "where's Rory?"' Olazábal recalled in a *Sunday Telegraph* interview with Oliver Brown a week later. 'He was teeing off in bloody twenty-five minutes. Once we got hold of him on the phone and he was updating us on where he was on the road, telling us that he was in a police car and going really fast, we knew by 11.05 a.m. that he was going to make it.'

The police at the exit from the interstate that led to the Medinah Country Club had done their job. Lights flashing, the Crown Vic pulled on to West Lake Street, less than two miles from the course. They had made good time on the freeway as Rollins had gunned the squad car north. There were still 15 minutes until McIlroy was due to tee-off.

'If we hadn't had the lights on it would have taken another ten minutes from the highway junction,' McIlroy said later. But with the lights, they bypassed the traffic and sped onwards to the course. Soon they began to see the neat surburban homes with their manicured lawns that signalled the approach to the main entrance to the course. Some of the homeowners had set up opportunistic yard sales in the hope of attracting the custom of some of the thousands of passing spectators. Others had set up stalls selling cookies and home-made lemonade.

Those glimpses of small-town America must have seemed like visions of paradise to the young Irishman as he realized he was nearly at his destination and that he was going to make it. There were conflicting estimates of how much time McIlroy had to spare when Rollins dropped him off at the clubhouse. Some said eight minutes. Some said 11.

It did not matter. It was enough time for McIlroy to pull on his golf shoes and take a couple of practice putts on the green on the other side of the bridge from the first tee. By now, word of his late arrival had spread among the packed galleries in the grandstands around the tee and the ten-deep crowds that lined both sides of the first fairway.

The US television networks and Sky already knew about his timekeeping lapse and the premature triumphalism that had gripped the supporters as they anticipated a crushing US victory had turned to a gloating kind of hilarity. They thought they sensed disarray in the European ranks. They thought they scented not just a victory, but a humiliation. They thought they were going to be able to laugh at McIlroy for years to come.

So as McIlroy walked over the bridge to join Bradley, who was already standing on the first tee, the mocking jeers began. There were stubborn cheers from the Europeans around the tee, too, but it was clear they were shaken by the story of McIlroy's dash to the course. The best they could manage really was relief. And they were drowned out by Americans who had made up their minds they were going to have an awful lot of fun at McIlroy's expense.

McIlroy did his best to brazen it out. As he turned towards the grandstands from the bottom step off the stairs that carried him down from the bridge, he walked into the wall of noise and held his arms out wide in a gesture that was intended to convey 'what's all the fuss about?' In the circumstances, it was a decent attempt at bravado. The American fans, though, were not discouraged.

Bradley shook McIlroy's hand warmly on the tee. He had been worried that McIlroy was late because he had had an accident or some other mishap had befallen him. McIlroy smiled again, a little wryly this time, and told Bradley the truth. Bradley smiled, too.

At the back of the tee, the former Barcelona manager, Pep Guardiola, stood waiting nervously with his wife and three children. He had been renting an apartment in Manhattan during his sabbatical from football and now he had found another way to make the most of his time off. Guardiola, who had fashioned such a wonderful team at the Nou Camp, had decided to stay with the McIlroy match to its conclusion. The best tend to follow the best.

The first two singles matches – Watson v Donald and Simpson v Poulter – had already teed-off and moved on. The atmosphere in the grandstands surrounding the first tee and among the galleries that lined the fairway was febrile. McIlroy tried to act as if everything was normal but his caddie, JP Fitzgerald, who had arrived at the course an hour earlier, thought McIlroy would be shaken. They both knew Bradley was the American star man. Fitzgerald advised McIlroy to try to stay with his opponent for the first six holes, recover from the trauma of his late arrival and then attempt to find a way to win.

On the first tee, McIlroy got a taste of things to come. Suddenly, every American fan thought he was Jerry Seinfeld. 'Still on Eastern Time, Rory?' one voice shouted out. There were guffaws all round. 'Miss your alarm, Rory?' another voice yelled. Cue more delighted laughter and jeers. McIlroy slammed his drive down the first but pushed it to the right edge of the fairway where it came to rest in a tightly bound coil of television cable. He set off after it and ran the gauntlet from the galleries.

The cheers and the noise on that first fairway was deafening, walls of sound converging from both sides and colliding somewhere above the heads of McIlroy and Bradley. It was like the noise an English football crowd used to make in the seventies and eighties, visceral and passionate, full of longing and desperation to beat a bitter enemy, making it feel as though sport could not get more intense and pressured than this. It made the hairs on the back of the neck stand on end.

Whenever there was a brief lull, the taunts about McIlroy's late arrival still came at him in a torrent.

'What's her name, Rory?' one voice boomed out.

'You sleep in, Rory?' yelled another.

'I got some Advil for you, Rory,' another screamed, suggesting a hangover cure.

'Want a cup of coffee, Rory?' the next guy shouted.

McIlroy smiled sardonically a few times and then started munching on an energy bar as he strode down the centre of the fairway.

'Healthy breakfast, eh, Rory?' someone called out.

McIlroy had kept smiling until then. He got to his ball and, in the presence of a rules official, bent down and began to uncoil the television cable as gingerly as if he was about to cut the wire on an explosive device.

'Wake up, Rory,' another voice yelled.

McIlroy smiled again. He was waking up all right. So was the European team.

Somewhere out on the course, an alarm bell was ringing. It was just that the US players and their supporters could not hear it yet.

16 Europe on the charge

When he got to the first green, McIlroy took a look at the scoreboard. He knew every part of José María Olazábal's plan was going to have to work for Europe to stand even an outside chance of overhauling the US. He knew that four players at the top of the order all had to win, the middle order had to pick up its share and the tail had to wag furiously.

The scoreboard told him that up ahead, Luke Donald had taken an early lead against Bubba Watson in the first match. Watson had gone through his usual routine on the first tee. When he approached his ball to take his tee-shot, the crowd had fallen silent out of habit. Watson looked around at them quizzically. They got it. They started screaming like banshees. Watson took his pink driver and hooked his tee-shot into the galleries down the right side of the fairway.

McIlroy also saw that Ian Poulter, in the second match against Webb Simpson, was all square after the first hole. Many had noted the purposeful figure of Tiger Woods striding behind Simpson after he had taken his drive at the first. Woods was not out until last, placed there by Davis Love in case of an emergency, but even so, no one could remember him doing something like this to support a teammate before. Maybe he wanted one last chance to get to Poulter.

The first indications were that, if that was Woods' plan, it wasn't going to work. Poulter left his second shot just short of the green at the first. He pitched his third shot over the fringe and watched it bobble and run. It bumped into the flagstick and dropped into the hole. Simpson hit a fine long putt for birdie to halve the hole. What a start.

McIlroy took it all in. He was calming down. He had got used to the crowd making fun of him now. He halved the opening hole after a delicious chip gave him a two-foot putt for par. The 2nd was halved, too. Bradley's drive smashed into a tree on the 3rd but he rescued a half. He started trying to wind the crowd up again as he walked to the 4th, desperate to rediscover the highs he had enjoyed with Phil Mickelson.

But for the first time all weekend, Bradley started to struggle. He found himself in a bunker at the 4th and botched his attempt to get close to the pin from the sand. When McIlroy got his third shot close, Bradley conceded it. He was a hole down. Maybe McIlroy had been right when he guessed the Americans might struggle when they were taken out of the comfort of their partnerships.

McIlroy seemed different in the singles. There was a steel about him. Forget the late arrival. He was already over that. The crowd kept trying to wind him up but they were only succeeding in making him want to silence them by playing great golf. McIlroy had played well enough over the first two days without ever catching fire. Now he looked utterly formid-able and his opponent sensed it.

Bradley whipped the crowd up again as he walked to the 5th tee. McIlroy drove deep into the woods and his ball came to rest beside a gravel path. He tried to reach the green with his second but found a bunker. Bradley then hit his shot into the same trap. McIlroy's escape was much better and he had an 18-inch putt for birdie. Bradley needed to make a 15-footer to save the hole. He drained it and went wild, whirling his arms to gee up the crowd. He was still 1 down, though.

At the 6th, McIlroy left his second shot just short of the green again but his touch from that range had been more beautiful than ever all weekend. If the American fans were filled with foreboding when he prepared for his third shot, they were right to be. His chip was delicately, wonderfully judged. It trickled unerringly into the hole. Europe was now 2 up.

McIlroy took another look at the scoreboard. Donald was playing masterfully and keeping Watson at bay. He had gone 2 up after four holes and after eight the margin was still the same. Like Bradley, Watson was struggling to recapture the momentum he had revelled in on Friday and Saturday in his partnership with Simpson.

Simpson and Poulter were locked in a battle royal. Poulter had gone two down at the 4th but had forced his way back into the game. By the 8th, the match was all square again. Simpson had shanked his tee-shot. It made it obvious quite how much he was feeling the pressure and Poulter admitted later it had given him great heart. Poulter had shaken off the lethargy that had gripped him at the start of the match. So far everything was going as well as Europe could have hoped.

It was too soon for the Americans to be feeling a hint of anxiety. As McIlroy went to the 7th tee, Michael Jordan lit up a big cigar and loped on down the fairway. Guardiola, doing his best to remain inconspicuous, looked nervous and jumpy, every bit as engrossed in the action as he had been when he was standing on the touchline at the Nou Camp. Michael Atherton,

Justin Rose pulls off a remarkable singles victory over Phil Mickelson by winning the last two holes.

Rose celebrates as Mickelson prepares to congratulate him. Mickelson had earlier applauded Rose when he sank a monster putt to win the 17th.

ANDREW REDINGTON/GETTY IMAGES

Opposite: Martin Kaymer came out of the shadows at Medinah to stand over the putt that would win the Ryder Cup for Europe.

Right: Kaymer lets the putter fall against his left leg as he celebrates sinking the 6ft putt that completed Europe's astonishing comeback.

Below: Rory McIlory rushes on to the 18th green after Kaymer's putt to join the melee of deliriously happy European players around the German.

The scoreboard tells its own story at Medinah, the story of how the US got tangled up in blue.

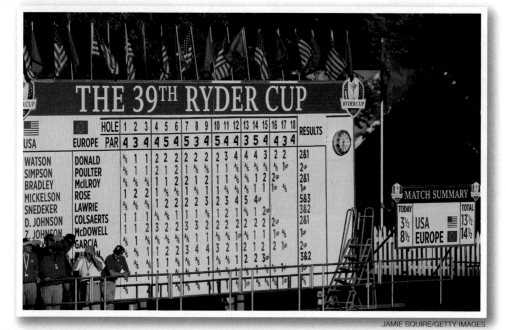

THE 39TH RYDER CUP

USA	EUROPE	HOLE	1	2	3	4	5	6	7	8	9	10	11	12	13	14	15	16	17	18	RESULTS
		PAR	4	3	4	4	5	4	5	3	4	5	4	4	3	5	4	4	3	4	
WATSON	DONALD																				2&1
SIMPSON	POULTER																				2up
BRADLEY	McILROY																				2&1
MICKELSON	ROSE																				1up
SNEDEKER	LAWRIE																				5&3
D. JOHNSON	COLSAERTS																				3&2
Z. JOHNSON	McDOWELL																				1up
	GARCIA																				2up
																					3&2

MATCH SUMMARY

	TODAY	TOTAL
USA	3½	13½
EUROPE	8½	14½

Tiger Woods sees the funny side as he greets McIlroy at the conclusion of the competition. Americans who hoped he might win more than half a point weren't laughing.

Poulter, the hero of the hour, screams victory while Lee Westwood prepares to drench him in champagne.

McIlroy drapes himself in a Northern Ireland flag, his happiness mixed with relief that he had made it to the course in time.

Molinari, who halved the final singles match of the day with Woods and so gave Europe outright victory, bows to the Italian flag.

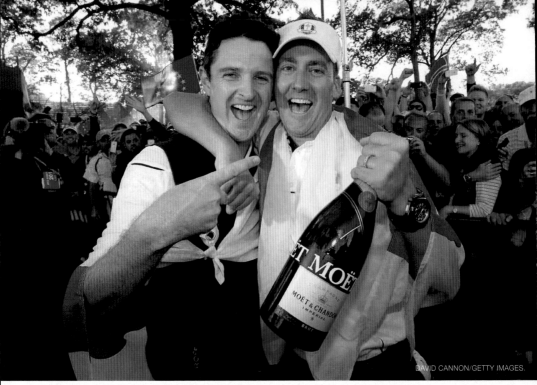

DAVID CANNON/GETTY IMAGES.

Poulter and Rose, Europe's best perfomers, get into the party spirit as they begin to realize what they have achieved.

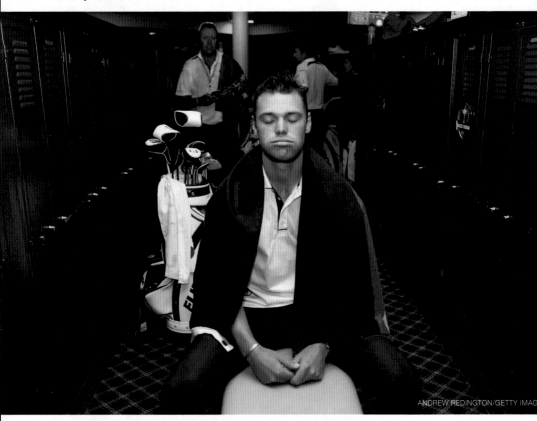

ANDREW REDINGTON/GETTY IMAG

The enormity of what he has done, the enormity of quite how much there was to lose, starts to sink in for Martin Kaymer.

DREW REDINGTON/GETTY IMAGES

Above: After
the American
supporters had
streamed away
from Medinah in
disbelief, European
fans cheered their
heroes by the 18th
green.

DAVID CANNON/GETTY IMAGES

Kaymer gets his hands on the Ryder Cup as McDowell and Rose pay
homage to the act of nerve that clinched their victory.

MIKE EHRMANN/GETTY IMAGES

Olazábal savours a victory that a few hours earlier had seemed like an impossible dream.

Nicolas Colsaerts, Darren Clarke, Lee Westwood, José María Olazábal, Francesco Molinari, Paul McGinley and Miguel Ángel Jiménez arrive back at Heathrow with the booty.

JAN KRUGER/GETTY IMAGES

the former England cricket captain, had begun to walk with this match, too, now.

Bradley was still struggling. McIlroy missed a fine opportunity to go 3 up at the 7th when he pushed an eight-foot birdie putt right and at the 8th Bradley made him regret it, sinking a 12-foot birdie to win his first hole of the day and cut the deficit. He pumped the crowd up again and windmilled his arms. They did not need a lot of encouragement. They were still filled with the spirit of invincibility that came with their overnight lead.

McIlroy hit a brilliant wedge approach to within five feet at the 9th and went back to 2 up. Bradley, whose pre-shot routine was growing more and more idiosyncratic the more the pressure built, grabbed another shot back on the 10th. On the 12th, McIlroy started munching on a hefty sandwich as he strode down the fairway, a final nod to his late arrival. But he missed the green with his second shot and Bradley stole another hole back. Suddenly, the match was all square.

Both men survived the natural amphitheatre that is the 13th hole with thousands of spectators clinging to the hillsides around the green on both sides of the lake. They were all square going to the 14th but Bradley cracked again and this time there was to be no way back. He hit his second shot into the trees and his third into a bunker. He could only make par. McIlroy had a four-foot putt for birdie. He rattled it in and was back in the lead.

McIlroy went for the kill. He hit a beautiful approach shot to the 15th and left it three feet from the hole. Bradley missed his birdie putt and now McIlroy was 2 up again with three to play. McIlroy drove into the trees at the 16th but saved par and halved the hole. He was 2 up with two to go. He had nearly done it.

The waters of Lake Kadijah glistened below him as he stood on the 17th tee. The wind swirled and McIlroy waited for a while to let it drop. His tee-shot was safe and perhaps 20 feet from the hole. His birdie putt rolled to within a couple of feet, and he tapped in for par. Bradley had an 18-foot down-hill putt to extend the match. It was close but it died to the right just short of the hole and finished a few inches adrift. The game was over.

Bradley, one of America's invincibles, had been taken down. The rookie who could do no wrong on Friday and Saturday, who had been burning with so much energy that he was like the battery for the US team, had finally run out of power. His defeat was a blow to the Americans. Love had hoped that he more than anyone would have the confidence and the form to head off a European charge straight away. Love knew the dangers of Europe gaining momentum. He thought Bradley would derail them but he was wrong.

McIlroy's victory was a huge boost for Europe. The world number one had done his job. He had beaten the man who had become America's totem. He had turned a late arrival and what might have been an incident that made Europe a laughing stock into a great triumph. How good did McIlroy look now, arriving at Medinah 11 minutes before his tee time and still beating America's best player.

Another thing appealed to European supporters about McIlroy's victory. They said it was the kind of thing Ballesteros would have done. Everyone talked about escapology with Ballesteros. Well, how about this. Rushing to the course in a police car, coming close to being disqualified, eating your breakfast on the way round and winning the game. The Ryder Cup had never seen a piece of escapology like that before, even from Seve.

'I calmed as soon as I got here,' McIlroy said by the side of the 17th green. 'If I warm up for forty minutes, it's a long time for me anyway. I only warmed up for twenty-five minutes before

I won the PGA this year. So getting here late was probably a really good thing. I didn't have to think about it too much.

'When I got the match-up with Keegan, I liked it. I liked the idea of playing one of their strongest players and going out there and putting a point on the board early for the team, and I was able to do that. Now we'll see what happens.

'There was a lot of positivity in the team room last night, especially the way we finished. Winning those two points in the last two games was crucial. We've tried to carry that momentum into today, and we've sort of done that. But we need to go out and support the boys now in the middle of the order and see if we can get them home as well.'

McIlroy was not the first to put a point on the board for his team. In fact, two others had beaten him to it. First Donald had closed out his match with Watson, although not without a scare. He had been 4 up with four to play when Watson launched a furious late rally. The American birdied the 15th to win the hole. Then he chipped in at the 16th to reduce Donald's lead to two holes.

There were more nerves on the 17th when Donald hit his tee-shot long and left and into a bunker. The Europeans following the match were getting alarmed. Some still remembered Mark Calcavecchia's notorious Ryder Cup collapse against Colin Montgomerie in 1991 when he blew a four-shot lead in the last four holes and thought he had lost the Cup for his team.

Donald did not let that happen. He clipped his shot out of the sand to within a couple of feet of the hole and sealed his par. Watson needed to hole his pitch shot to extend the match. He couldn't do it. Donald had put Europe's first point on the board. Watson had been stilled. America's human dynamos were running out of steam. It was 10–7.

'I don't know what I would have done going down eighteen if it had gone that far,' Donald said. 'The nerves were starting to build and Bubba was putting some serious pressure on me. He made some great birdies and the chip in on sixteen was unexpected but in this competition, you've got to expect that.

'It was a big honour for me that Ollie had enough trust in me to go out and get that first point for Europe. That means a lot to go out first and lead the team, and I did what I had to do. I felt a lot of responsibility. I think Ollie expected a lot from me. He rested me on Friday afternoon for a reason: to be strong for the end of Saturday and today, and I delivered two points. Hopefully it's good enough. The boys are going to have to push hard, but I'm going to go out there now and cheer them on.'

The other match that had finished by the time McIlroy beat Bradley was one of the results that few would have anticipated, one of the results that Europe needed if they were to have a real shot at a record turnaround: Paul Lawrie's dismantling of Brandt Snedeker 5&3. It was the fifth match out but it was second to finish. Lawrie's point made it 10–8.

In many ways, Lawrie was the forgotten man of the European team. That had seemed to be his fate throughout his career. He never got the credit he deserved for his Open victory at Carnoustie in 1999 even though he had shot a final round 67 to force his way into the play-off. The headlines went to Jean Van de Velde's meltdown on the last. Lawrie's victory was written off as a fluke.

The fact that he scored 3½ points in his Ryder Cup debut at Brookline a couple of months later was also largely forgotten amid the European defeat and the controversy surrounding the behaviour of the American team. But under the fiercest pressure, playing with Colin Montgomerie, who was the target of so much bile, Lawrie played superbly.

He endured plenty of lows after that. The second Major never came. He went nine years without winning on the Tour and, worst of all, people began to look at him as a hard-luck story. He was the guy that had never been able to deal with winning a Major. The guy who had gone downhill fast from there.

'There is not a golfer or sportsman in the world that does not go through poor spells and questions if they can do what they are supposed to be good at again,' Lawrie said in the build-up to Medinah. 'In golf things can change so quickly. It's amazing how in January you can be hitting it like a dog and missing every cut and then in February, March you have one good week and you are off. This game can be a torture like that. You hit a poor shot and you have to wait before you can put it right. You might hit two in a row, make a double and you are thinking, "Man, I just can't do this any more." That's how it is.

'Two things changed for me. Doing Ryder Cup commentary at Celtic Manor in Wales had a huge impact. Sitting there talking about something you think you should be playing in was very motivating. I had not been to a Ryder Cup since the one I played in, just watched on television. The whole thing was massive. I was thinking, "I want to be part of that again. I think I'm capable if I just knuckle down."

'Around about the same time, my eldest son beat me. It sounds a bit silly, and I was proud of him, but I was thinking that I should not be getting beaten by a fifteen-year-old kid. So I did what I had to do to start climbing the rankings again. A lot of hard work, basically. I have had only a couple of weeks when I have missed cuts. I have not been known in my career for that kind of consistency. I have always been the type of player who finishes fourth or fifth one week then a missed cut. That has changed so it's been nice.'

It had taken Lawrie 13 years to get back to the Ryder Cup and when he and Peter Hanson were being pulverized by Watson and Simpson on Friday afternoon, some of the Scottish journalists in the Media Centre were shaking their heads sadly and saying his return would last only 13 holes. Lawrie spoilt that line slightly by extending the match to the 14th where he and Hanson eventually succumbed 5&4.

He played with Nicolas Colsaerts on Saturday afternoon and lost again, narrowly this time to Dustin Johnson and Matt Kuchar. He had played well in patches in both defeats. Then he was drawn against Snedeker in the singles, the guy who had just won the Tour Championship and the FedEx Cup. It was another point the Americans expected to win easily.

It didn't turn out that way. The first three holes were halved but then Lawrie accelerated away. He chipped in at the 4th and eagled the 5th. He was 3 up by the 11th, won the 12th, too, and took a five-hole lead at the 13th. Lawrie closed it out on the 15th, winning 5&3. Olazábal had expected Donald and McIlroy to win but no one had really expected Lawrie to beat Snedeker and certainly not so convincingly.

It was a vital point. A huge point. It was a great fillip for Lawrie, too. He was properly part of things now. He had made his contribution and he had struck an important blow for his team. Somewhere, his son was watching, feeling a new pride in his dad. His victory changed things. It made people begin to wonder for the first time whether the Americans might have to fight for the Cup after all.

McIlroy's victory over Bradley brought the scores to 10–9. Attention switched back to Europe's hero, Poulter, who was still locked in his battle with Simpson. It seemed almost too much to hope that he could do it again, that he could pull off yet another triumph against the odds against the reigning US

Open champion. The match looked like it was going down to the wire.

As the match reached the 17th, Poulter had not held the lead at any stage. After Simpson's shank on the 8th, the American had regained his composure and gone back into the lead with a birdie on the 10th, only for Poulter to level things up at the 12th. For the next four holes, the match had remained all square, although Poulter had to produce a miraculous recovery from the woods on the 16th to halve the hole.

But at the 17th, Simpson blinked again. His tee-shot flew through the back of the green into the bunker and he could only get his recovery to within 12 feet. Poulter's tee-shot landed on the green. His birdie putt missed but it was an easy par. Simpson had to hole a difficult putt to ward off falling behind for the first time in the match. He couldn't do it. He pushed it to the right. Europe was 1 up with one to play.

It wasn't over, though. It was Poulter's turn to feel the heat. There was mania all around him on the 18th tee and he sliced his shot wide into the woods where it came to rest beside one of the corporate marquees. Poulter held his nerve. 'This Ryder Cup is not for the faint of heart,' he said later. 'Sometimes you just have to buckle up and hit a shot.' He blasted his second shot over oak trees and it landed on the green, stopping 13 feet from the hole.

Simpson was on the fairway but the situation got to him again. Remember what Love had said about standing on the 18th fairway at The Belfry in 1993, so nervous that he wanted to be sick? That was what Simpson was feeling now. His second shot betrayed his tension and rolled 50 feet beyond the pin. He hung his head. He knew it was almost over. He had one last chance but his birdie putt slid right. He knew he could not win the hole so the match was over. He conceded Poulter's putt. Poulter had won.

Poulter's Ryder Cup record now read a remarkable 12–3–0. It was the fourth Ryder Cup in which he had won his singles match. In that part of the competition, he was yet to lose. Nobody was thinking about Poulter's individual statistics at that moment, though. Everyone looked at the score ticker. It read 10–10. The scores were level.

'It's unbelievable,' Poulter said by the side of the 18th. 'That was a really tough day. Webb played pretty solid today. I didn't have my best early on and I managed to stick in it. Looking at that leaderboard right now, we have an unbelievable chance. We have a chance from somewhere we've never been before, and I'm so proud of the guys that have gone out early and managed to secure their points.

'I love this format. I love the team. Everything about it. I just love it. I've got Seve on my arm, Seve on the bag, we've got Ollie. It's pretty special. The boys who are still out there have just got to somehow come good. The team spirit last night in that team room was unbelievable. The buzz, the electricity, I just felt something might be possible today, and you know, we've never done it before. They have done it to us in '99, and who knows, it could be the greatest turnaround of all time for Europe.

'I didn't play my best stuff in the early holes today but I knew, you know what, if the guys early could pull me through, then we have got a great chance and that's exactly what's happened. We have got up, we won all those early matches, and we just need Rose to somehow do something coming up the last and I tell you what, that board looks very different.'

17 Tangled up in blue

For the first time, the Europeans thought they actually had a chance. For the first time, they dared to hope. Not just the abstract hope they had felt in the team room the night before when Olazábal had invoked the memory of Ballesteros and breathed belief into each and every one of his players as he went through the singles line-up. Now there was real hope.

It was still fragile, though. Things had gone almost impossibly well so far. The first four points won on Sunday had all gone to Europe. Some of the biggest American names had already been taken down. Defeats for Bubba Watson and Keegan Bradley had been grievous blows. They had sapped the home team of morale, drained it of some of its energy and robbed it of its certainty.

But the reality was that the US were still favourites. The day might have started freakishly well for Europe but the US still needed only 4½ points from the 10 matches still out on the course. The match was entering a crucial phase. It was still too early to predict the scores in the final games but a survey of the middle order matches identified one crucial match in particular.

Nicolas Colsaerts was down to Dustin Johnson in the sixth match out. It had been all square for a while but Johnson was about to win three holes in a row to seal America's first point of the day and put them 11–10 up. Graeme McDowell, who had been struggling all week, was heading for defeat, too. He was down to Zach Johnson and never even had a share of the lead. Peter Hanson, who had had a wretched Ryder Cup, was four holes down to Jason Dufner at the turn in the ninth match.

In Europe's favour, Lee Westwood had finally found some form and was cruising to an impressive victory over Matt Kuchar. But it was clear that Europe would have to win two matches that were currently finely poised in the middle of the order. Only then would it be even worth starting to consider whether Europe's weakest players, Martin Kaymer and Francesco Molinari, could somehow shock either Steve Stricker or Tiger Woods in the final matches. Those swing matches, the next crucial contests, were Phil Mickelson against Justin Rose and Jim Furyk against Sergio García.

Mickelson–Rose was one of the highest quality singles pairings. Rose had beaten Mickelson 3&2 at Valhalla in 2008 but this Mickelson seemed like a different proposition. He had been energized by partnering Keegan Bradley and it had begun to feel as though he was the leader of the team. He was determined not to be on the losing side at a Ryder Cup yet again.

But Rose was a better player than he had been in 2008, too. In fact, he was finally earning recognition as one of the world's elite players. There had been spells when it seemed he was destined to be best remembered as the teenage amateur who holed his approach shot at the 72nd hole of the 1998 Open at Royal Birkdale to secure a tie for fourth place.

For a while, it seemed as if he might be forever trapped in that moment. He turned professional straight after Birkdale but missed the cut in his first 21 events. For a while, he became a curiosity, the kid hobbled by premature fame. But he earned his first European Tour card in 1999 when he finished fourth at the qualifying school and gradually his career took off.

For some time, it seemed like he might just be an ordinarily brilliant golfer, a fine player but not someone who contended for the top prizes. He always had a reputation as one of the nicest, most approachable guys on the Tour and sometimes that was used against him. He was too nice, too shy, to be a winner. No nasty streak, people said.

But Rose won the 2007 Order of Merit on the European Tour and was ranked in the world top ten for 34 weeks between November 2007 and July 2008. And six months before Medinah, he won his first World Golf Championship event at the WGC-Cadillac Championship at Doral, in Florida. It was the biggest win of his career. And the week before the Ryder Cup, he finished second to Brandt Snedeker at the Tour Championship, moving his world ranking to a career high of 5 at the age of 32.

Rose gave some of the credit to his run of form in the build-up to Medinah to little-known North Carolina-based putting coach David Orr. 'David is into the science of putting and that's how I like it,' Rose said. 'I like to understand why something works and something doesn't. I was down about my putting around June and July but really believe I have made great strides since. It's obviously been great the last few weeks and the great thing is I'm doing it under pressure.

'I'm more consistent than I was back in 2007, my game has fewer faults. That's because of all the work I've done with my swing and in the gym. I understand more about my game now and, of course, the professional game in general. I'm a better all-round player with a better all-round mindset.'

His match with Mickelson had swung first one way, then the other. Rose was 2 up after the first two holes. Mickelson levelled things by winning the 4th and the 5th. Rose went ahead at the 7th, Mickelson hit back at the 8th. Rose went ahead against at the 9th but Mickelson squared things up at the 11th. And then, at the 14th, Mickelson took the lead for the first time and it seemed as though he might be about to close the match out.

It had become obvious by then that this could be one of the Ryder Cup's decisive matches. If Mickelson won, the story of Medinah was likely to be of Europe's heroic failure and how they gave America an almighty scare but came up short. Mickelson stayed 1 up until the 16th and it seemed briefly as if he had gone dormie when he sank a 10-foot putt for par.

Rose had an eight-foot putt to save the hole, save his prospects of winning the match and, probably, keep alive any chance Europe had of pulling off a miraculous comeback to win the Ryder Cup. Rose stood over the putt for a while and then rolled it into the centre of the hole. He clenched his fist and let out a yell. He was still alive. Europe could still cling to hope.

The 17th brought an incredible swirl of emotions for both players and both teams. The atmosphere there was as loud and as fervent as it had been anywhere during any stage of the competition. As the scoreboard turned blue, there had been a growing realization that the outcome of the Ryder Cup was now in doubt. The excitement had reached fever pitch.

Rose's tee-shot at the par-three landed 40 feet from the flag but at least it was on the putting surface. Mickelson missed the green. He had a difficult lie in the rough on the bank at the back but his genius is with any sort of lofted club and when he chipped on, the ball headed straight for the hole. Mickelson saw its path. He knew that if the ball dropped he had probably won the match. He knew that, after so many times being the Ryder Cup dunce, this might just be his moment to be the guy who won it. He started running after the shot as it rolled, his arms in the air in celebration. It seemed to be heading straight for the centre of the cup but somehow it stayed out. There was a collective groan from the American supporters. Rose conceded the putt.

Now it was his turn. If he could get close enough to halve the hole, that would be a consolation. He would still have a chance of securing half a point at the 18th. It probably wouldn't be enough but what else could he do? He hit the putt and stood back and watched. It rolled and it rolled and it rolled, travelling across the contours of the green, turning left to right down the slope towards the deep blue lake. And then it dropped.

Rose stood there. He did not clench his fist or punch the air. He did not leap or shout. He just stood there, puffed out his chest and looked around the green, nodding his head. He was like a boxer climbing into the ring, staring at his opponent. The drama had become unbelievable. It was the best of the Ryder Cup so far. At the back of the green, Mickelson watched in amazement. When Rose's putt dropped, he smiled and applauded and gave Rose the thumbs-up. Then he headed towards the 18th tee. The match was all square.

That sequence, at that stage of the Ryder Cup, with everything suddenly in the balance, was about as good as sport gets. Everyone on that green sensed the genesis of a miracle. It happens sometimes in sport, that feeling that a higher power is at work. Perhaps it is just momentum. Perhaps it is just confidence. That's not what the European players thought, though. They were very clear about who was leading this charge. They believed it was Ballesteros.

No wonder Rose took a deep breath before he hit his drive on the last. This could be one of the defining moments of his career. His ball flirted with the rough on the left of the fairway.

Mickelson was also down the left. But when Mickelson's second overshot the green, Rose landed his about 12 feet from the flag. Mickelson chipped on from the back of the green and gave himself a good chance of making par. Now Rose putted to win the hole, to win the match, to put Europe level with the US at 11–11, to stretch belief, to send the European fans wild. His birdie putt was firm and true. It disappeared into the hole. Rose had done it. He had come from one down with two to play to winning the match. In the moment of his victory, as the Americans reeled, it felt like anything was possible.

Rose is not usually emotional but he was emotional now. 'As soon as I holed that putt, as soon as I came off the green, my first thought was "Seve",' he said. 'You know, he's been an inspiration for this team all week long, and who knows, if something crazy happens today, I know that we are going to be looking upwards.

'Having an eight-foot putt to halve the hole on sixteen, to dig myself out of that game was incredible. I felt like we needed that point, as well, to have any chance. On the seventeenth, Phil was looking confident like he was going to make that chip. Then he missed and I buried it on top of him and that was one of the best feelings of my life.

'And then the eighteenth. Well, now I know how Ian Poulter feels. I had a glance down and looked at my left sleeve where we have the silhouette of Seve. That's the kind of stuff he would have done today.

'Those putts on sixteen, seventeen and eighteen are the three biggest putts I've ever made back to back in my career under pressure. When I was standing over the putt on the eighteenth, I was shaking a little bit and I said to myself, "Rosey, this is what the whole week could come down to for you. If you miss it, you might feel disappointed, but if you make this putt, it's going to be a good week for you." And I just did what I had to do.

'Now I am going to get back out there, support our boys, put the pressure on the Americans. If they hang on, good luck to them but we have given it everything today. I'm proud of the boys so who knows, a bit of fortune and this could be an incredible day.'

The action was moving fast now. Things were changing. It was hard to keep up. Zach Johnson closed out his 2&1 victory over Graeme McDowell to put the US 12–11 up. Westwood sealed his triumph over Matt Kuchar by 3&2 to make it 12–12. 'At one point, I had a putt from about a foot and I was still nervous,' Westwood said. 'In fact, I was shaking like a leaf.'

There was everything to play for now. There was no longer any attempt at trying to conceal the fact Europe could do this. It was there for them now. They still needed a lot to go their way but suddenly all the pressure was on the Americans. It was starting to look like one of the biggest chokes in sports history.

There was panic in the press room, too. It was bang on first edition deadline for many English newspaper writers. Pieces that had been written on the basis of an emphatic American victory were being hurriedly rewritten or changed via stress calls direct to sub-editors.

One had written a piece praising the new breed of young American golfers who were set to take the world by storm. That was going to have to go.

Another had written a piece criticizing José María Olazábal and including the sentence 'his captaincy left much to be desired'. As despair gripped the journalist, a senior colleague offered him some advice. 'Just change it from "his captaincy left much to be desired" to "his captaincy left nothing to be desired",' he said. Thus spake the voice of experience.

The Ryder Cup was too close to call now. The focus switched to the denouement of the critical match between Furyk and García. It had been a desperately close contest but just as with Rose and Mickelson, when the players arrived at the 16th green, the US held a one-hole lead.

García nearly rolled his bunker shot into the hole for a birdie, leaving Furyk with a 15-foot putt to win the hole and go dormie. Furyk sent the ball on its way, followed it with eyes and then raised his arms in triumph. He thought it was in but it caught the lip, rolled right around the hole and stayed out. Furyk hung his head. García said later he thought that was the moment that broke Furyk's heart.

At the 17th, the tension was unbearable again. The waters of Lake Kadijah looked dark and foreboding as they rippled between the players and the green. The place was turning into an American graveyard and Furyk knew it. His tee-shot found the bunker. García landed in the centre of the green.

The momentum was moving so quickly with Europe now it took the breath away. Furyk splashed out of the bunker but his ball raced 10 feet past the hole back towards the water. García's birdie putt was close enough to be conceded. That meant Furyk had to bury his uphill putt to save the hole. He pushed it right. The European players and their partners who had gathered by the side of the green in a huge group threw their arms in the air and let out something between a shriek and a roar. The force was with them.

Furyk's drive at the 18th found a bunker 170 yards from the green. Hearts were in mouths everywhere. Could he reach the putting surface from there? Could Europe possibly win another match in which they had been one down with two to play? If they did, how hard would it be for the US to recover from the shock?

Furyk made the green. Just. But his ball rolled down off the back edge and came to rest about 50 feet from the hole. García was on the green 25 feet from the pin. Furyk took an age to weigh up his putt. He walked from his ball to the heart of the green three times. He knew there would be a left to right borrow on it but he did not read it quite correctly or get the pace right and it went eight feet past the hole. García's putt to win the match stopped a couple of inches short.

Now it was all on Furyk. He had bogeyed the 17th. Now he had an eight-foot par putt to halve the hole and the match. He knew if he didn't make it, he would be called a choker. He knew if he didn't make it, the Ryder Cup might slip away. He knew that he might be at the heart of one of the most famous failures in golf history. He hit the putt. It rolled right of the hole.

García had won. Europe had won. They were 13–12 ahead. It was the first time in this Ryder Cup that they had been in the lead. They needed one more point from the three matches left out on the course to retain the trophy.

But there was a cost. It was hard to see what happened next. Whatever one's allegiances, it was difficult to see the effect something like that can have on a man who believes he has failed, who believes he has let his team down when it mattered most. It remained one of the most haunting images of Medinah.

When his ball rolled past the hole, Furyk bent double, as if he was in agony.

18 Langer, Kiawah, Kaymer

When Martin Kaymer reached the 16th tee, José María Olazábal walked up to him and spoke with great urgency.

'We need your point,' the European captain said. 'And I really don't care how you do it. Just deliver.'

Kaymer was pleased. He told himself he could handle it. 'I liked it,' he said. 'It was very straightforward. That's the way we Germans are.'

By then, Jason Dufner had beaten Peter Hanson 2 up. The Ryder Cup was tied at 13–13. Europe needed one more point to retain it. The US needed a point and a half to regain it. Francesco Molinari and Tiger Woods were fighting out the last singles match and it was too close to call. Olazábal believed Europe's hopes of pulling off the greatest fightback in Ryder Cup history rested on Kaymer beating Steve Stricker.

Kaymer's round so far did not exactly inspire confidence. He had hit his tee-shot at the 13th into Lake Kadijah and lost the hole, allowing Stricker to bring the match level. He won the 14th then lost the 15th. The match was all square again when Olazábal caught up with him at the 16th tee.

Olazábal may have struck the right note with Kaymer when he spoke to him but the European captain must have wondered whether the German was going to come through for him. Kaymer had had a wretched weekend. He was playing poorly and he was psychologically fragile. He was probably the last person Olazábal wanted in this position but he had had to front-load his singles line-up to try to force Europe back into contention. He had to play Kaymer somewhere.

Kaymer had won the US PGA title in 2010 and had briefly become the world number one in 2011 but he had begun to struggle for form as the Ryder Cup approached. Olazábal had left him out of the Friday morning foursomes but paired him with Justin Rose for the afternoon fourballs. They were comfortably beaten by Dustin Johnson and Matt Kuchar. Kaymer did not play well.

On Saturday, Olazábal told him he was leaving him out of both sessions. He would not play again until the singles. Kaymer was distraught. But he also recognized that he had not been in the right frame of mind when he had played on Friday. He saw how motivated his teammates were and worried that he was out of step.

'Saturday was very difficult for me,' Kaymer said. 'I wanted to prove I could do better than I'd done on Friday because on Friday I didn't show good golf. But I didn't get the chance to play on Saturday which was fair enough. It was José María's decision, and we have to respect that, but I definitely wanted to show him that I can win a match here.'

Kaymer texted Bernhard Langer on Friday night and asked if they could meet on Saturday morning. Langer – who was in town doing some work for one of the Ryder Cup sponsors – was a hero and a mentor to Kaymer. The two men were the only Germans ever to win a Major and Langer was a Ryder Cup stalwart who had captained Europe at Oakland Hills in 2004. He had also missed the six-foot putt that lost the Ryder Cup at the bitterly contested War on the Shore at Kiawah Island in 1991.

'I wanted to talk to him about the Ryder Cup,' Kaymer said, 'because I felt like my attitude . . . I would say I was not as inspired as I should have been. We talked a little bit about a bunch of stuff, and he has been a fantastic role model for me, and he's always there if I need him. And that is very rare to have someone like him that you can ask whenever you need to.'

Kaymer felt reassured by the chat with Langer. His attitude was better on Sunday. He arrived at the course determined to atone for what had happened on Friday. He made two birdies on the front nine against Stricker and was 1 up at the turn. Every time he looked at the scoreboard, he realized there was a growing chance that, rather than being a dead rubber, his match might be the decisive clash of this Ryder Cup.

Olazábal's urgent words did not have the desired effect immediately. Kaymer promptly put his approach shot to the 16th in the bunker shielding the front of the green. Stricker, who had played three times at Medinah already without winning a point, did the same. The hole was halved.

The pressure now was unbelievable. These men had the Ryder Cup in their hands. Both knew their teams desperately needed them to win. Stricker hit his tee-shot at the 17th safely over Lake Kadijah. It landed on the green and came to rest on the back fringe. Kaymer hit over the water, too. He was on the green left-centre but further from the hole than Stricker.

Kaymer putted for birdie. It twisted off to the left as it began to die and finished five feet from the hole, well outside gimme range. Stricker chipped from the back of the green and his shot rolled left as it slowed, too. He was about the same distance from the hole as Kaymer. Stricker putted first now. The ball kissed the right side of the lip and stayed out. Stricker bowed his head.

Now it was Kaymer's turn. This to go 1 up. This to allow Europe, who had seemed in such a hopeless postion when dawn broke, to put one hand on the Ryder Cup. This little putt to bring the completion of one of the greatest comebacks in sporting history a giant step closer. Kaymer stood over it, lifted his putter back and hit it. It rolled and it fell. The Americans supporters around the green fell silent. The Europeans went crazy. It was bedlam. Europe were ahead. Stricker needed to win the final hole just to give the US a chance of regaining the cup.

Behind them, Woods was about to go 1 up on Molinari at the 17th. As long as Kaymer could somehow hold off Stricker on the 18th, though, that didn't matter. If Kaymer could do as Olazábal had asked him and win his point by whatever means necessary, then Woods would be an irrelevance, a ghost stranded out on the course unable to influence the winning and the losing of the Ryder Cup. If Kaymer lost the hole, though, Woods, the competition's great under-achiever, would get his shot at glory. As he went ahead at the 17th, he must have been thinking that redemption was nigh.

Kaymer hit his tee-shot at 18 off to the right and into a fairway bunker. Initially, the sight of its trajectory was met with alarm and groans from the European contingent. But the ball was not plugged. It had a decent lie. There was no reason why Kaymer should not make the green. Stricker hit second. His drive went up the middle of the fairway.

Kaymer got a clean contact off the sand and landed his approach on the green. It bounced and rolled towards the left-centre. Stricker's approach was not as good. His ball rolled well past Kaymer's on to the upper level of the green, deep into shadow. He was about 40 feet away.

The tension was so great, it felt like it was difficult to breathe. Stricker putted first but misread it completely. The putt started left and stayed left. It did not turn right at all. The American was left with an eight-foot putt for par. Kaymer was about 30 feet away. If he could get down in two putts, Europe would retain the Ryder Cup.

Kaymer rolled his birdie putt towards the hole through the shadows and the little pockets of fading sunlight that dappled the green. It looked good. There were cheers. But it went right of the hole by a foot and rolled six feet beyond it. Rory McIlroy and Luke Donald were standing side by side at the edge of the green. When they saw where the ball had ended up, they shot each other nervous glances. There were murmurs of apprehension all around.

First, Stricker had to putt for par. He took an age weighing it up. He backed off the putt twice, squatting on his haunches, bending the peak of his cap to try to funnel his vision and read the hole better. Eventually, he stood over it and putted. It went dead centre. He picked the ball out of the hole and clenched his fist. He knew that he had, at least, placed Kaymer under horrendous pressure.

Kaymer stared at the putt. Something was bothering him. His putt was six feet from the hole. Just like Langer's had been at the War on the Shore. Kaymer looked again. There was a blemish on the putting surface between his ball and the hole. There had been a pitch mark between Langer's ball and the hole in 1991, too. The coincidences were piling up. The omens were not good.

'I was only six when Europe lost at Kiawah Island but I know it was talked about a lot afterwards,' Kaymer said. 'When

I went behind my putt I saw a footprint and for half a second Bernhard crossed my mind. But I thought, "Okay, it's not going to happen again, it's not going to happen again." And to be honest with you, I didn't really think about missing. There was only one choice you have; you have to make it. If you stick to the facts of the putt it was the easiest one you could have, uphill, inside right. We have that putt a million times so I just thought, "Step up, make it."'

So he stepped up. He took his time, too. He bent down and squeezed the rim of his cap as well. Then he was decisive. No backing away from the putt. He stood over it and hit it. Time seemed to stand still. So much had gone into this moment. So much energy, so much hope, so much emotion. And then it dropped. It was over. Europe had retained the Ryder Cup. The Miracle of Medinah was complete.

Kaymer stood up straight and allowed the putter to fall against him. Then he clenched his fists and shook them for all he was worth as millions of people screamed at their television sets in explosions of joy. After a couple of seconds, Kaymer ran over to the side of the green and leapt into the arms of Sergio García. His teammates mobbed him and hugged him. The celebrations began in earnest. The Americans looked stunned and bemused.

Olazábal was not among the throng. He was waiting with Molinari back on the 18th fairway. He had stayed out of it all in case Kaymer had lost the hole. He wanted to be there for Molinari if he needed him. He understood what had happened but he was trying to keep his emotions in check. He muttered some instructions in Molinari's ear then walked away a few paces and started crying.

Molinari and Woods played out their match. Woods had no interest in it. He missed a four-foot putt to win the hole and then conceded Molinari's three-foot putt. The match was halved. It was a noble gesture from Woods although the book-makers cursed him. It meant that instead of the competition being tied, as it would have been if Woods had won the final point, Europe had now won 14½ to 13½. The odds on a European win at the start of the day had been 25–1. Woods' act of chivalry cost the bookies millions.

Kaymer was still being mobbed. He was still lost in wonder at what had happened. He had been an afterthought until today. Now he had won a favoured place in Ryder Cup history. He was the man who sealed the greatest comeback there had ever been.

'It feels a little strange being called the hero,' Kaymer said. 'It was such a fine line between being the hero or the biggest idiot. I was very surprised how many people came up to congratulate me. I made the last putt but at the end of the day I only got one point while other guys inspired the team a lot more than me. What Ian Poulter did on Saturday is difficult to put into words. I think he at least deserves more credit than anyone else on the team.

'I was inspired talking to Bernhard yesterday morning but I got even more inspired by Poulter yesterday afternoon. I told Ian just now that I thought about him on the sixteenth this afternoon. When I had to make a par putt on sixteen, I thought, "Come on, if he can do it, you can do it, too, so show him that he inspired you for that special event." Ian should be part of the Ryder Cup for ever.

'And you know, when I stood over that final putt on the eighteenth, I was not that nervous. I was so very controlled because I knew exactly what I had to do. But if you ask me now how that putt went and how it rolled, I have no idea. I can't remember. When it went in, I was just very happy, and that is something that I will remember probably for the rest of my life and hopefully I can talk about when I have some grandchildren one day.'

Olazábal listened to what Kaymer said as they stood by the side of the 18th green. Tears rolled down the captain's cheeks.

'This event is so special,' Olazábal said. 'Look at twelve men like this, giving their hearts and trying to win the trophy. You don't see this anywhere else in any other tournament. They have given you their best, one hundred and twenty per cent. They have sacrificed themselves for the benefit of the team.

'I cannot explain today. The guys did a wonderful job. Maybe they knew how much it meant to me. Last night in the meeting I told them that I really believed they could do it. The pairings were well balanced and they just believed in themselves. That's why we are here as winners.

'When I saw that we had a chance this afternoon coming down the stretch I was very emotional. I started to think of the possibility of winning. My boys have done an unbelievable job.'

Then Olazábal turned away for a second before he could resume.

'I have a few thoughts for my friend Seve,' he said. 'This one is for him.'

19 The hollow men

The players of the US team looked like hollow men when they filed into the interview room in the Media Centre. Their expressions were blank. They stared down. It was as if they could still not quite believe what had happened, that a competition they thought they had won had slipped away in such agonizing fashion.

When they took their baseball hats off, they looked strange. The lower half of their faces were tanned where the peak of the cap had not protected their skin from the sun. The top halves, especially their foreheads, were pale and wan. It made them look slightly eerie. Melancholic and full of regret, it was as if a row of ghosts had sat down to talk.

Tiger Woods sat nearest the exit. He wore an expression that said he was in a particularly foul mood. Then again, he often appears to be in a particularly foul mood, especially when the press are around.

But there is always an image in this miserable ritual of Ryder Cup defeat that lingers longer than the rest. In 2008 it was Olazábal losing his dignity when he was asked a reasonable question by Paul Hayward. In 2010 it was Hunter Mahan sitting behind the table, desperately trying to get words out but succumbing to the overpowering guilt of the belief that it was he who had lost the Ryder Cup.

This time, the reaction that most searingly conveyed the pain of losing so narrowly and the shame of having surrendered such a convincing overnight lead belonged to Jim Furyk. Furyk is a decent, level character but it was obvious he was close to the edge after the way Sergio García had stolen the match from him in the last two holes.

The demons were gnawing at him, telling him that just a half against García would have been enough. Just halving either the 17th or the 18th would have been enough. Just sharing the spoils with the Spaniard would have made him the hero. Just getting that precious half a point would have transformed his year and washed away the pain of throwing away a winning position at the US Open a few months earlier.

Instead, he had to live with the fact that in eight Ryder Cup appearances, he had now been on the losing side six times. He had not got the job done. He had not done the thing that Love had picked him specially to do. The skipper had sent out his experienced guys last in the belief that if Europe had mounted a comeback, men like Furyk would stand steady and remain resolute and strong. Furyk had not been able to deliver.

Then the question came. An American journalist in the middle of the cavernous room asked it. 'You had some tough finishes in events this year,' he said to Furyk. 'Can you describe the difference as an individual versus this kind of maybe letting your teammates down or your captain who picked you to be on the team?'

Furyk paused for a beat. It was like he was absorbing a punch. The room went very quiet. Sometimes that happens when a hard question is asked and a sportsman's emotions are raw and everyone knows they must be hurting. It was the same at the Athens Olympics in 2004 when someone asked a censorious question to a tearful, vulnerable Paula Radcliffe about why she had failed to complete the women's marathon.

Eventually, Furyk answered. 'Well, first of all,' he said, his voice trembling slightly, 'I would gather that you probably haven't been on a team to ask that question. Losing the US Open, losing Bridgestone, I'll be honest, it's been a very difficult year but if you had been on a team or if you had been on this team, I've got eleven guys, I've got a captain, I've got four assistants that I know will pat me on the back.

'They know how I feel. They understand how I feel. You know, we came here as a team. We wanted to win the Ryder Cup as a team and we didn't do it but we are going to leave here as a team. And I've got eleven guys here and I've got a captain and I have four assistants that have my back. As for your question about team versus individual, it's the lowest point of my year.'

It was a stirring, almost demagogic rejoinder, emotional and angry. But the thing that stayed with those who were there was the intensity the question unleashed in Furyk. And most of all, the fact that even after he had finished answering it, he kept his eyes trained on the journalist who had asked the question.

So the press conference moved on, Woods started answering a question about Ian Poulter and still Furyk was staring at the journalist who asked the question. This is not a man who ever loses control and yet he looked on the very edge of reason now. The journalist started to shift in his seat. He was certainly not meeting Furyk's gaze.

This time, it was not Paula Radcliffe who came to mind but Mike Tyson. Some of the journalists in the room had been at the Hudson Theatre in New York in 2002 when a press conference to announce Tyson's world title fight with Lennox Lewis had degenerated into a mass brawl on the stage that ended with Tyson screaming at the audience of journalists.

One of the newspapermen, an American boxing writer who wore a bowler hat and called himself Scoop Malinowski, shouted back at the stage. 'He's an animal,' Malinowski yelled. 'Put him in the circus. Put him in a straitjacket. He belongs in the circus.'

Malinowski was only about seven rows back and Tyson fixed him with a demonic stare. He launched into an expletive-laden tirade about the sexual indignities he would like to visit upon Malinowski and how those indignities might teach him to like Tyson more. To love him, in fact. Tyson seemed to be preparing to launch himself into the audience so he could get at Malinowski, who had suddenly gone very quiet and soon made a rather hasty exit.

Furyk may have very little in common with Tyson but in those instants in the interview room, it seemed he was so angry that he might be about to walk down off the stage and confront the journalist who had asked the question. He kept staring at him for what seemed like an eternity but was only really a little over a minute. Finally, he looked away.

The search for blame is the inevitable subtext of these losers' press conferences at the Ryder Cup. Usually, the finger begins to point towards the captain or the most high-profile player. This time was no different. Most of the questions were aimed at Woods, who had had another desperately disappointing Ryder Cup, and Love, the captain of the team that had just succumbed to what the American press suggested the following morning was the biggest choke in Ryder Cup history.

Love stayed steadfastly true to his philosophy and his principles. He was dejected, obviously, but somehow he managed to remain unruffled. He did not indulge in recriminations. He did not criticize anyone else. He was gracious towards the Europeans and heaped praise on the players who had come so close to winning the trophy back for America.

The questions kept coming at him. Had he maybe become complacent when the US had finished play on Saturday with such a commanding lead? Had he approved of Woods conceding a half to Francesco Molinari on the final hole? And, most persistently, did he now accept he had made an error in resting Phil Mickelson and Keegan Bradley on Saturday afternoon when they were sweeping all before them?

Love began to answer the question about Mickelson and Bradley. He said he accepted that there were things he might have done differently with the benefit of hindsight. He made a couple of vague allusions to players wanting to be rested and others who wanted to play five matches.

It was obvious that Love was ready to take the blame if that was what was required. He knew that was part of the job. Or it was as far as he was concerned. The most important thing for him was to behave in the correct way and the honourable way. 'I'm going to second-guess myself for a long time,' he began to say. 'I could have done a lot of things differently but I'm proud of—'

A couple of seats away, Mickelson sensed what was happening. He sensed Love was offering himself up. He leaned forward and interrupted Love. 'Hold on, Davis,' he said. Love didn't hear him at first and kept on talking but Mickelson persisted. 'Hold on one sec, Davis,' he said. Love stopped talking and Mickelson spoke in the manner of a man who has suddenly decided to make a dramatic courtroom confession.

'As far as playing Keegan and I,' Mickelson told the journalists, 'you need to hear something. Keegan and I knew going in to Saturday morning that we were not playing in the afternoon and we said on the first tee, "We are going to put everything we have into this one match because we are not playing in the afternoon."

'And when we got to the tenth hole, I saw Davis there and I went to him and I said, "Listen, I know you are going to get pressure to do this because we are playing so good but you are seeing our best and you cannot put us on in the afternoon because we emotionally and mentally are not prepared for it."

'I told him we had other guys that were dying to get out there and that we had put everything into our morning match and that we wouldn't have anything later so we had to stick to our plan. So you cannot put any of the blame for that on Davis. If anything, it was me because I went to him on the tenth and said that to him.'

It was a startlingly similar speech to the one Mickelson had made at Celtic Manor in the equivalent press conference two years earlier. That time, he sought to deflect the blame away from Hunter Mahan. This time, he was willing to take the rap instead of Love. Love looked across at him appreciatively. It was a noble gesture.

Mickelson has a great generosity of spirit. It is one of the reasons why he is so popular with golf fans wherever he goes. He makes time for people. He signs autographs for fans. He acknowledges them out on the course and interacts with them when he can. The further Woods has fallen from grace, the more Mickelson has come to be seen as his opposite.

Mickelson's gestures of self-sacrifice, his apparent readiness to take one for the team, only enhance that image. They widen the gap between him and Woods even more. Woods sits there with a scowl, snapping out terse answers and exuding an overriding desire to get the hell out of there. Mickelson auditions for Joan of Arc and the role of world ambassador for his game.

On occasions like this when they are sitting on opposite sides of a dais, Woods snarling in defeat, Mickelson turning a shattering defeat into a personal triumph for a stand-up guy, the contrast between the two most talented American golfers of their generation is never more fascinating. Woods may well come to be recalled as the greatest golfer who ever lived but it is Lefty who will be remembered with the greater affection.

So Woods sat in the corner at Medinah, brooding. There were more questions about his decision to concede the putt on the final hole. He knew there would be. Press conferences containing a phalanx of British journalists always had the potential to be more unpredictable than regular dates on the US PGA Tour and Woods already knew that Dick Turner was among the group sitting right in front of him.

Turner is a veteran British sports journalist who is not afraid to ask hard questions even in the rarefied world of golf press conferences. Over the years, he has repeatedly challenged Woods on issues that others have shied away from. Sometimes, it feels as if no one is asking the question because they are waiting for Turner, who has worked for a variety of outlets including the *Daily Star*, to do it for them.

Woods is an intimidating presence in a press conference. Not as openly aggressive as someone like Sir Alex Ferguson or Tyson but there is an impatience simmering just below the surface. His aggression does not manifest itself in an explosion of anger, more in a concentrated froideur. Difficult questions, anything that strays from a narrow path of inquiries about whether he hit a five- or a six-iron for his approach to the 14th, are cuffed away without any real attempt at analysis.

In that context, Turner's questions are perfectly legitimate as well as deliciously entertaining. When he gets at Woods, there is always a feeling that a naughty child has sneaked into the room and is flouting all the conventions. Woods is all about control so to be there when somebody refuses to play by his rules is refreshing. Woods fights against giving any sort of insight into his personality but sometimes Turner's questions provoke at least the spark of a reaction.

Some journalists, from both sides of the Atlantic, scoff at Turner's questions to Woods. Some say they are disrespectful. Some seem to think they do not chime with the gentlemanliness of the sport. Some seem to regard them as uncouth. But some of the same journalists use Turner's questions and Woods' responses to them as the basis for their articles. And their newspapers write their headlines on the back of them.

At the 2004 Ryder Cup at Oakland Hills, after hapless American captain Hal Sutton Jr had disastrously paired Woods with Mickelson in the lead fourballs on Friday morning and the foursomes in the afternoon, Turner had asked Sutton why he had sent out his two weakest players first. Sutton fumed about that. Everyone else smiled.

There is a faintly theatrical element to Turner's delivery sometimes and when Woods is in a good mood or trying to present an amiable face to the world, he manages a wry smile when Turner begins his question. Other times, he listens with a face like thunder. At St Andrews in 2010, Woods faced the press in Britain for the first time since the scandals about his personal life had engulfed him. Some asked gentle, sympathetic questions. Turner was not one of them.

'Tom Watson has said you need to clean up your image on the golf course,' Turner told Woods. 'Many of us have heard you use the "F" word, we've seen you spit, we've seen you throw tantrums like chucking your clubs. Are you willing to cut out all those tantrums and respect the home of golf?'

Woods managed a very thin smile. 'I'm trying to become a better player and a better person,' he said.

At Augusta the following year, Turner pursued a similar theme.

'We have a foul-mouthed footballer back in the UK called Wayne Rooney,' he said. 'He has been suspended for foul and abusive language. Would you like to see suspensions coming to golf for the same thing?'

'You like to ask questions each and every year, don't you?' Woods said.

Turner did not disappoint at Medinah, either. As the American players sat there and the inquest into their spectacular final-day collapse began in earnest, Turner asked the first question, the question that was on everybody's lips.

'Tiger,' he said, 'why did you concede Molinari's three-foot putt on the last? Had he missed it, it would have been a tied match, which is a lot better from a US perspective than a one-point defeat.'

Woods spat out the answer. 'It was already over,' he said. 'We came here as a team. This is a team event. And the Cup had already been retained by Europe, so it was already over.'

Woods managed a brief blind-side dig at Poulter, comparing him to Colin Montgomerie and suggesting, without actually saying it, that he could not play as well in the Majors as in the Ryder Cup. Then he was asked again about how he had felt being stranded out on the course with Molinari when the competition had already been decided.

'Yeah, well, I've been in that situation before,' Woods said, hinting at the frustration that had been churning inside him. 'If you guys remember, in 2002 at The Belfry, I was in that same position against Jesper [Parnevik] on seventeen when [Paul] McGinley won the Cup.

'So it's a tough spot to be in because you know you've got to finish out the match even though it's useless because our team didn't get the Cup and they did. So eighteen today was just, "Hey, just get this over with", and, you know, congratulations to the European team. They played fantastic today and they deserve the Cup.'

The bookies may have been upset with Woods for his gesture towards Molinari but the American public and journalists showed no real appetite to try to turn him into a scapegoat. Most accepted that even though he had had another miserable Ryder Cup in terms of the points he had scored, the defeat was not his fault. Others on the US side had played worse than him. If anyone was in the firing line, despite Mickelson's intervention, it was Love.

The Americans seemed to find it particularly hard to believe that they had collapsed in the singles. It was the segment of the competition in which they were supposed to excel. Two years ago, at Celtic Manor, they had mounted a charge of their own on the final day which so nearly allowed them to retain the Cup.

So Love's captaincy, widely admired over the first two days, now came under the microscope. Once again, his attitude was criticized. He was told he had been too laid back, too nice, too humble, too consensual, too generous. Whatever Mickelson had said, not at least to have allowed Bradley to go out again on Saturday afternoon was also held against Love.

The performances of his captain's picks also came under fire. It was pointed out that other than Dustin Johnson, who won three points with no losses and no halves, Love's selections backfired. Jim Furyk, Brandt Snedeker and Steve Stricker won only one match (Furyk and Snedeker's narrow win in the

Saturday foursomes) between the three of them all weekend. They lost the other eight. It was a desperately poor return. 'That's how you get the greatest collapse in Ryder Cup history,' Michael Collins, ESPN's senior golf analyst wrote, 'and that's why you get the blame.'

Others were keen to back Love by reminding his critics that five of America's most dependable players, men who had combined to win six of their eight partnered matches with an overall margin of 22 holes, were the men who lost the opening five singles matches on Sunday. Not much Love could do about that.

Love addressed the festering issue of Bradley and Mickelson again in a candid, moving column he wrote in the early hours of the morning after the defeat by Europe. He explained that his intention had been to play each of the two-man teams he had established before they arrived at Medinah three times over the four fourballs and foursomes sessions. 'Golfers tend to be creatures of habit,' he said. 'We like order. I was trying to provide order.'

Poor Love. The agonizing had begun. The second-guessing, the wondering, the self-flagellation that curse the losing captain of each and every Ryder Cup was already setting in. On the eve of Medinah, Nick Faldo had admitted that the stigma of leading Europe to defeat at Valhalla after being such a successful player was something that had continued to haunt him.

There was something particularly cruel about that fate. In the modern Ryder Cup, so many others are clamouring for the honour that it is the norm that the captain only gets one shot at the job. One shot at it and if it goes wrong, if someone else's putt lips out or someone else's drive goes into the trees, you are consigned to history as the man who lost the Ryder Cup.

It is a heavy burden to bear. 'The bottom line is that it was a tough experience and very tough for me to deal with afterwards,'

Faldo told Derek Lawrenson in the *Daily Mail* when he finally brought himself to talk about how things had unravelled in 2008. 'I wanted to leave with a win, I wanted to have that feeling because you know you only get one chance and I am a winner. Sure it left a scar. There's still a small one there, even now.'

And now Love was wrestling with the same demons. Now even the man who is outwardly so calm, so hard to ruffle, the man who more than most players on the tour looks as if he has discovered the formula for contentment, was sitting on a veranda outside the team room at Medinah in the early hours of Monday morning, pouring out his words, searching for some sort of catharsis, being eaten up by what he could have or should have done.

'After three sessions we had a considerable four-point lead, with the team of Keegan Bradley and Phil Mickelson winning three times,' Love wrote. 'Fred Couples, another of my four assistants, said to me, "Man, that Keegan Bradley is on fire. Ride him all the way to the house."

'In other words, he wanted me to play the Bradley–Mickelson team again on Saturday afternoon in Session IV. I know a lot of fans and commentators were thinking the same thing. But Phil told me he was tired after three matches and wanted to rest for the Sunday singles. There was no reason to play Keegan with a partner with whom he had not practised. There was no reason to mess with the order.'

Love sat there for a while longer in his red, white and blue pyjamas. They had been given to each member of the team by Furyk's wife, Tabitha, as an attempt at a good luck charm. Payne Stewart, the American golfer killed when the cabin of his private jet suddenly lost pressure, had worn the same pyjamas the night after he had played in the US's highly charged comeback win in the 1999 Ryder Cup at Brookline.

Love sat there and worried about how he would cope with not being able to put things right. He thought about how later that day, the Chicago Bears would play the Dallas Cowboys in the NFL's Monday night game. He thought about how one team would win and one team would lose. And he thought about how they would get the chance to play again six or seven days later. But the next time the Ryder Cup would be played was at Gleneagles in Scotland in September 2014. The next time the US had a home game was two years after that. Love knew that the cast and crew in Scotland would be completely different and that in Ryder Cup golf, it's now or never.

Isolated incidents kept coming back to him, moments where he might have done something to alter the course of history, moments when, in his own mind, he had failed. They bounced around in his mind, torturing him and teasing him, taunting him that after almost two years of preparing for the job, he had been found wanting when the crunch came.

He was haunted by the idea that, perhaps, he, too, had choked. That he had frozen when his team needed leadership in the white heat of the final few holes and everything was crumbling. He had been unable to shore his team up, unable to save them as they began the vertiginous fall towards calamity in the closing couple of hours of the match. He had been gripped by a paralysing powerlessness.

'I said to Scott Verplank, one of my assistants, "Which match do I watch?",' Love recalled. 'You want to do everything, and you really can't do much of anything. You're a baseball manager, and every one of your pitchers is on the mound in the ninth inning of a Game Seven.

'Jim Furyk walked by me after losing the seventeenth hole. The Ryder Cup on the line. I wanted to say something, but what could I say? He walked by me with that fierce game face of his on, and frustratingly I found myself saying nothing. I turned to Jeff Sluman, another of my assistants, and said, "Well, that was brilliant." But the fact is, in golf it's better to err on the side of saying too little than too much. And I'm sure there were times I said too much.'

Love began to agonize about his singles line-up next. Had he got his order right? Was there anything he could have done to have stopped Europe getting out to such a tremendous start at the top of the order? It was that start that gave them a momentum they rode all the way to the finish.

And what about putting Woods at the bottom of the order? Stone last. For all his Ryder Cup travails, Woods has a more than respectable record in the singles. He feels comfortable in the singles. In the singles, he's finally back to not having to worry about anyone but himself. And there's also the small matter of the fact that he is one of the greatest players ever to pick up a golf club. Wasn't it madness that he had been stranded out on the course again while the Ryder Cup was being won and lost?

'We loved our Sunday line-up,' Love said. 'I say "we" because this team functioned as a group. I was a players' manager. I listened to my assistants, the caddies, the wives and most particularly the players. We reached a consensus on every big decision we made, from the four players I hand-picked for the team to our Sunday order. Tiger said, "Put Strick and me at the end. I don't think it will come to us, but if it does, we'll be ready." Tiger has won three times this year. He's the greatest match-play golfer ever. He's the greatest golfer ever. Hearing those words from him was enough for me.'

Well, it turned out Strick wasn't ready. And Tiger wasn't exactly roaring either. There was nothing that Love could do about that, really, although Stricker's poor showing was an endorsement for those who had maintained all along that Captain Love's picks had erred too much on the side of conservatism and experience. The players in whom he put his faith struggled to validate his opinion of them.

Some time that night, Love's phone began to whirr. It was a text from Woods. He was stuck in traffic on the way to the airport. There were road works on the freeway and he had taken several wrong turns trying to navigate his way around the snarl-up. He gave Love the impression it had been a stressful journey. 'A perfect ending to a perfect day,' Woods wrote in the text.

But as Love told himself he had to abandon his soul-searching and attempt to get some sleep, he did his utmost to summon some positive conclusions from everything that had happened. That is Love's nature. That is what his upbringing taught him. He sees the best in people. He has learned from bad things that have happened to him. He stays positive.

So now, he drew comfort from the fact that he had given his all and that he and his team had kept their dignity in difficult circumstances. 'I feel a sense of satisfaction,' he wrote. 'I gave it my all. (My team gave it more.) I feel a sense of emptiness. (Losing stinks.) I feel a sense of pride. My team handled its 48 hours of prosperity without ever being cocky and handled its Sunday defeat with true graciousness. From start to finish, in good times and bad, José María Olazábal's European team showed nothing but class. Golf is better now than it was last week.'

Love was right about that. If Britain's successes at the Olympics had made people want to climb on a bike, for instance, and get out on the road, or if the Paralympics had made people re-examine their attitudes to disability sport and to disabled people in general and even to the terms we have used to define them, then what happened at Medinah made new legions of men and women want to take up golf.

It had been the best of sport, two teams fighting themselves to a standstill, a competition fought out in an atmosphere of rare intensity, a contest that went right down to the wire because the two teams were so evenly matched and wanted to win so badly and a Ryder Cup that was enhanced by unwavering grace in defeat of the vanquished captain.

It is easy to be magnanimous in victory but it is an awful lot harder to treat a luckless defeat in quite the same fashion. That is a gift that only the best possess and Love proved even in the moment of America's loss that he had class that knew no bounds. It is hard to think that he could have been any more inspiring if America had won than he was now that they had lost.

He continued by writing that he would carry the defeat of Medinah with him always, but that the defeat would not drown out all the good memories he had of the week. These included the inspirational Greatest Hits film featuring the Chicago Bulls, which Michael Jordan played for the team to remind them that the players' job was not only to win matches, but also to help their teammates become better players. Love went on to lay the blame at his own feet, saying 'if you need to blame somebody for this loss, blame me.' He acknowledged that the job of the captain is to help his team win, and that he'd have to live with the frustration that this didn't happen at Medinah. He concluded, poignantly, with a note to his players: 'We came to Chicago as a team and left as an even more united one. We'll be bonded for life by what we did at Medinah. Being your captain has been the greatest honour of my golfing life.'

20   Poults Clause

When, finally, it was the turn of the victorious European team to speak to the media, they filed in one by one, taking their seats behind the table on the dais where they had been answering questions all week. Justin Rose first, then Lee Westwood, Peter Hanson, Luke Donald, Ian Poulter, Nicolas Colsaerts, José María Olazábal, Rory McIlroy, Francesco Molinari, Sergio García, Paul Lawrie and Graeme McDowell. They sat and stared out at their audience, beaming.

There was some of the usual tomfoolery that accompanies victory press conferences like this when the players have already been celebrating for a couple of hours. Westwood seemed intent on chatting to Rose while the press conference was going on, leaning back in his chair, knowing that Rose is a meticulously courteous man with the media, trying his best to make him laugh.

When he got bored with that, he had a chat with one of the photographers standing by the wall. He appeared to be asking him to move away but it was good-natured. It was all good-natured. How could it be anything else? Paul Hayward asked García a question. García started to answer it and then a cocktail was handed to him for him to pass down the line. Then another, then another, then another. The answer was a long time coming.

There were plenty of questions to McIlroy, of course. When someone asked him about his journey to the course, Westwood tried to imitate the sound of a police siren. García jumped in, too. So often, he has looked a disconsolate figure on the golf course these last few years but now he was ready to make fun of himself and his troubles.

There was a time, he said, when he had experimented with not warming up before a round. He said he had recommended it to McIlroy. 'The best thing about it is you always come out to the course with the right attitude,' García said, 'because it doesn't matter how bad your shot is on the first tee; it's the best shot you've hit that day.'

Next, somebody asked Kaymer whether he had thought about Langer's missed putt at Kiawah Island in 1991 that had lost the Ryder Cup for Europe.

'I did,' García said, before Kaymer could answer.

Golf's answer to the Comedy Club went on for a few minutes more.

Colsaerts was asked what his thoughts had been when he had lined up one of his long birdie putts on Friday afternoon.

'Like I said the first day, man, you go with what's in your pants,' Colsaerts said.

'Well said, dude,' García added.

'Yeah, I liked that, dude,' said Westwood.

The next day Westwood and some of the other European players were criticized for their behaviour. 'It was a very difficult occasion to manage and I thought it was disrespectful,' PGA of America spokesman Kelly Elbin said. 'Westwood was hammered. Maybe the conference needs to be staged a lot earlier.'

There was very little to be offended about. The American media are used to more staid press conferences from their players rather than the kind of light-hearted japes Westwood often gets involved in. And anyway, hammered or not, Westwood delivered the best line of the day. He knew who everyone had come to see. He knew who the hero of the hour was. He knew everyone had come to praise Poulter.

'We have actually revised the qualification for next time,' Westwood deadpanned. 'It's nine spots, two picks and Poults.'

Everybody laughed. Westwood was encouraged.

'Poults Clause,' he added.

Poults Clause. How right that sounded on that Sunday night in Medinah. How right that sounded after everything Poulter had achieved over three inspired days. He had played four and won four. At various times, in various formats, he had taken down 14-time Major winner Tiger Woods, reigning US Masters champion Bubba Watson, 2007 Masters champion Zach Johnson and reigning US Open champion Webb Simpson.

He cut a swathe through the American team. He was irresistible. More than anyone, he won the Ryder Cup for Europe. More than anyone, he wrought the Miracle of Medinah. So when the press conference finished and the European team began to file out, a posse of journalists headed straight for where Poulter was standing and asked him to stay just a little longer.

Poulter was happy to talk. What a sweet moment this was for him. What a validation. Sure, he had excelled at Ryder Cups before but never like this. He had scored four points at Valhalla in 2008, too, but he had been on the losing team that year. He had never quite been the headline act before but this time there was no one to touch him. Not the man who holed the winning putt, not the world number one, not Tiger, not Bradley, not Bubba. No one.

He was, as several commentators pointed out the following day, deep into Colin Montgomerie territory here. A man who has never quite been able to nail one of the Majors but who is transformed into a golfing Superman during the Ryder Cup. A man who can fall prey to his vulnerabilities when he is playing on his own but who is lifted to new heights by the spirit of playing for a team.

A man like Woods regards the personality traits exhibited by Montgomerie and Poulter with barely disguised scorn. He only sees weakness. Those who are more drawn to team sport see something else. They see a kind of nobility in what Poulter did at Medinah that you cannot find in any other event in golf.

As he sat up there on the dais, Poulter did his best to analyse what turns him into one of the greats of the game for three days every two years. He talked about how his love of football gave him a keener appreciation of the team ethic. He talked about the motivation that comes from rejection. He even talked about being humiliated in the classroom as a child.

When the journalists crowded round him, he knew what was coming. Not just an examination of how he did what he did at Medinah but how he could translate it to the Majors. It used to be the same agenda with Monty. The subtext of the conversation was that this was all very well but could it act as a catalyst for finally winning one of the big ones.

It is a strange line of questioning in a way. Even as we are asking them, we are revelling in the fact that we have just seen one of the greatest sporting events of the year, something to be mentioned in the same breath as the Olympics, the Paralympics, the Tour de France and Andy Murray's victory at the US Open tennis. And yet the questions suggest the Ryder Cup is somehow subservient to the Majors.

If Woods ever wins a 15th Major, no one will stand up at

the post-tournament press conference and say: 'So, Tiger, can this act as a catalyst for you improving your miserable record in the Ryder Cup?' If anyone asked that, Woods would give them his most withering look and one of those scornful smiles he has perfected.

'That is Poulter's contradiction,' Martin Samuel wrote in the *Daily Mail* that week. 'He is just short of the talent to be in the class of Rory McIlroy, and his greatest strength, a screaming, half-mad desire to triumph by will alone, has always proved too draining mentally and physically to withstand four days at Augusta, Muirfield or beyond.'

Poulter seemed to recognize that as he sat on that dais. He talked briefly about the weariness he had felt and then banished in the first two holes of his singles match. 'I was a little flat at first in the singles,' he said. 'I chipped in at one, but I was tired and really struggling to get anything going. Being there on your own is tough sometimes. You need someone on there to give you a kick up the arse, but I didn't have that person and it made it difficult.'

For a few minutes, the joy of victory receded and he fell into an earnest contemplation of what drives him and what holds him back. He can be full of bluster but he is also one of the most reflective, articulate players on the Tour. And now he was adamant that what he had achieved at Medinah could not be reproduced at a Major.

'You can't do it, you can't do it, you can't do it,' Poulter said.

Somebody demurred.

'You can't do it, you can't do it,' Poulter said again.

Somebody offered a qualification.

'You can't do it,' Poulter said.

Somebody asked if he had ever tried.

'Of course, yes,' he said. 'Too draining. You can't do it.

'An event like this weekend could be a catalyst for me but you know what, these Ryder Cups might be my Majors, and that's fine. If they are, if this it, I'm a happy man. I've got more pride and passion to play in the Ryder Cup than I have to win a Major. I want to win a Major, don't get me wrong, I'd like to win all of them. I've been close and who knows, today might be that little changing factor to get me over that line. But if I don't win another golf tournament from here, today will go down as the highlight of my golfing career.'

Earlier, in the press conference, he had joked that he was going to take two years off and come back for the next Ryder Cup at Gleneagles in 2014. And now he was happy to admit he had a particular affinity for the event that he traced back to his love for football. A keen Arsenal fan, he was a regular at Highbury and the Emirates before he moved to Florida.

He began going to Orlando Magic games to get a fix of team sport but football was his first love. He still watches as many Arsenal games as he can on television and enjoys football banter with McDowell and McIlroy, who are both Manchester United fans. Anyone who follows him on Twitter knows how passionately he still feels about Arsenal.

He did not make it as a player. He was rejected by Arsenal's north London rivals, Spurs, when he was 14. But he was an Arsenal fanatic and like most football fans, he loved the crowd. He loved the noise and the atmosphere and the visceral feelings that being a supporter bring. He loved the theatre of it, the thrill of the interaction between players and fans, the way that you can lose yourself in the hubbub and the din. At some basic level, he said, the Ryder Cup was a substitute for all that.

'That's me, that's who I am,' Poulter said. 'I want to be the guy that's contributing to the team. In football, I always wanted to be the guy that scored the goal, just to do his bit, just to do enough to make a difference. I'm a team player, that's what I am. I like to give it 100 per cent. If I go down, I'm going to go down in flames.

'The Ryder Cup helps replace the team sports I miss from England. I was such a big football fan, I had that love of the game for so long. I miss the buzz, I miss going in the crowd and being a football fan. There is nothing like being amongst fifty thousand people all cheering on your team. I now know what it is like to be inside those ropes making those guys go nuts. It's truly inspiring. I do miss my football, but it's for the best. I am able to appreciate the passion of a Ryder Cup because it didn't work out for me in football.'

Poulter reminisced. He talked about the history teacher at Barclay School in Stevenage who had humiliated him because he was messing about with his golf clubs in class. He talked about lasting only a few minutes at his trial for Spurs before someone shouted out, 'Sorry, son, not good enough.' He talked about his competitive instincts and how he had inherited them from his dad, Terry.

'I've always been this competitive,' he said. 'Yes, in every form of sport I played, whether I was playing football, whether I was playing pool, whatever I was doing I was really competitive. My dad ingrained it in me, he always told me to play to win. So, yeah, I'm a bad loser. My dad's a bad loser. That's why I'm hard to play against in match play. That's why guys dislike me and want to beat me.'

Everyone remembered then the thing Jim Furyk had said before the tournament, about how no one in the American team wanted to lose to Poulter, about how the wild look in his eyes and the grandstanding to the crowd wound them all up.

He was the player the Americans most wanted to beat, the 'dick' who mooched a ride home on Tiger's plane, only none of them could manage to do it.

Poulter smiled at that thought and at the memory of how he had played the Americans at their own rabble-rousing game when he had encouraged the crowd to scream and shout as he was teeing off on Saturday morning against Bubba Watson and Webb Simpson. Mind games, they would call that in Poulter's beloved football. He just wanted to show he would not be intimidated.

'I feed off those guys,' Poulter said. 'If they want to be loud and create an atmosphere, that's great, let's go play golf. As long as it stays within the lines, that's fine. It was difficult at times out there this week.'

He said that some of the jeering and comments from the US fans had trodden a fine line between banter and unacceptable abuse. He said that aspect of the three days had been tough. He did not try to disguise that or deny it. But it never swayed him or put him off his game. He refused to be intimidated.

'That kind of thing fuels me,' he said. 'I might not have been born with the talent of some people, but I've got quite a big heart and I'm prepared to go out on the line. I've got as much confidence as anyone that has ever played the game and I've got as much confidence as anyone that I can hit the right golf shot at the right time.'

On this weekend of all weekends, that confidence was entirely justified. At Medinah, it was not even a case of Just Tiger and Me. Tiger was miles behind. So was everyone else. It wasn't Poulter and anyone. It was just Poulter. He was an inspiration to his teammates, to the millions watching and to his captain, José María Olazábal.

And that was how it ended with Poulter that night in the

Press Tent at Medinah. After all the self-analysis, he came back to the magic of what had just happened. He thrust himself back into the wonder of the Miracle of Medinah and tried to stay there a little while longer.

'Come on, it's fairy-tale stuff,' Poulter said. 'Can anyone believe what's just happened out on the golf course? I mean, seriously. We were dead and buried at one stage. On Saturday we were getting beaten badly and it was looking as if it was going to be humiliating. And then the team have all dug deep and have actually turned it around into the best Ryder Cup in history.

'To be part of a team is very special. This team's very special, and we've created history. I've never seen anything like this; it's amazing. To have Olly say what he said to me after that last round of golf will stay with me for ever. I can't tell you what it was but it was magic. It meant more than anything.'

The best guess is that Olazábal thanked Poulter for being the difference between winning and losing. Or perhaps it was something about Poulter being the Ryder Cup captain, too, one day, something that will surely come his way.

'I can't even answer that,' Poulter said, when he was asked if he would like to be Europe's skipper. 'I've got a few of these in me yet. If I ever get asked, of course I would do it. It would be an honour. But there are plenty who will step into Olly's position before I get there.'

Indeed there are. But the next man's first task is easy: invoke the Poults Clause.

AFTERWORD:
All men die, but not all men live

Ian Poulter didn't need to mooch a lift back to Orlando this time. The afternoon after the greatest triumph of his life, he travelled home in his own plane.

An hour or so after it had left Chicago, Poulter sent a tweet. 'Why does it feel like we just robbed a bank?' he wrote.

Lombard Deputy Police Chief Patrick Rollins had his picture taken with Rory McIlroy but tried to dodge the blame for costing America the Ryder Cup.

'The Ryder Cup was won on the golf course and not on the road,' Rollins said, 'but I am getting teased for not driving to the wrong golf course or getting a flat tyre.'

Tiger Woods apologized to the rookies in the US team for letting them down then went home to look after his two children, who were poorly with stomach bugs.

He said that caring for them kept his mind off what had happened for a few days.

Rory McIlroy flew to Turkey to play in the World Golf finals and lost all three of his matches. He earned £187,000.

Jim Furyk led going into the final round of the McGladrey Classic, his first event after Medinah.

He lost to Tommy Gainey, who shot 60 as he came from seven shots back to beat him. Furyk bogeyed the last.

Davis Love III had shared the lead with Furyk but also fell back. He said he could not get the Ryder Cup defeat out of his mind.

'It's good to get back to playing,' he said. 'It distracts me for four, five hours a day from thinking about what happened.'

Justin Rose beat Lee Westwood to win the World Golf Final in Turkey and set his sights on overhauling McIlroy in the Race to Dubai money list.

Bubba Watson went jet-skiing in Bermuda. Before he left, he wrote a tweet. 'Seve is/would be so proud,' it said.

After weeks of speculation it was confirmed that McIlroy had signed a 10-year £156m endorsement deal with Nike, confirming his position as golf's top star.

McDowell, Poulter, Rose, McIlroy and Westwood flew up from Florida to Chicago together en route to a tournament in China.

McDowell tweeted a picture of the Windy City as he landed. He put a caption on it, too. 'Scene of the crime,' it said.

In China, someone suggested to Woods at a press conference that he should follow Phil Mickelson's example at the next Ryder Cup and take a younger player under his wing.

'That's interesting,' Woods said.

Love was still trying to come to terms with how the Europeans turned things around at Medinah.

'I believe the soul of Seve Ballesteros, José María's mentor and the greatest of all Ryder Cuppers, truly inspired Europe on Sunday,' he said in an interview.

'There were tributes to Seve, who played golf as an artist and a matador, in the sky, on the yardage books and on the golf bags and uniforms of the European players.

'I know such inspiration is possible because I played with Payne Stewart on that '99 team at Brookline, the only other team to make up four final-day points in Ryder Cup play.

'Ben Crenshaw, our captain, in some indirect way made us feel his spiritual connection to his late teacher, Harvey (*Take Dead Aim*) Penick, and to Francis Ouimet, the Country Club caddie who won, improbably, the 1913 US Open.'

There were rumours in Europe that Olazábal was planning to take the Ryder Cup to Pedreña and place it for a little while at least underneath the magnolia tree in Ballesteros's garden.

He would not confirm the rumours but no one could forget what he had said when he stood on the stage at the end of the greatest Ryder Cup there had ever been.

He was looking at his team when he spoke and thinking about a man whose lust for life and passion for the Ryder Cup had endured beyond his death.

'All men die,' he said, 'but not all men live and you made me feel alive again this week.'

The 39th Ryder Cup, Medinah Country Club, Illinois, 28–30 September 2012

Results

Friday morning foursomes: USA 2–2 Europe

Jim Furyk & Brandt Snedeker lost 1 down to Rory McIlroy & Graeme McDowell

Phil Mickelson & Keegan Bradley beat Luke Donald & Sergio García 4&3

Jason Dufner & Zach Johnson beat Lee Westwood & Francesco Molinari 3&2

Tiger Woods & Steve Stricker lost 2&1 to Ian Poulter & Justin Rose

Match score: USA 2–2 Europe

Friday afternoon fourballs: USA 3–1 Europe

Bubba Watson & Webb Simpson beat Paul Lawrie & Peter Hanson 5&4

Keegan Bradley & Phil Mickelson beat Rory McIlroy & Graeme McDowell 2&1

Tiger Woods & Steve Stricker lost 1 down to Lee Westwood & Nicolas Colsaerts

Dustin Johnson & Matt Kuchar beat Justin Rose & Martin Kaymer 3&2

Match score: USA 5–3 Europe

Saturday morning foursomes: USA 3–1 Europe

Webb Simpson & Bubba Watson lost to Ian Poulter & Justin Rose 1 up

Keegan Bradley & Phil Mickelson beat Lee Westwood & Luke Donald 7&6

Jason Dufner & Zach Johnson beat Nicolas Colsaerts & Sergio García 2&1

Jim Furyk & Brandt Snedeker beat Rory McIlroy & Graeme McDowell 1 up

Match score: USA 8–4 Europe

Saturday afternoon foursomes: USA 2–2 Europe

Webb Simpson & Bubba Watson beat Justin Rose & Francesco Molinari 5&4

Dustin Johnson & Matt Kuchar beat Nicolas Colsaerts & Paul Lawrie 1 up

Tiger Woods & Steve Stricker lost to Sergio García & Luke Donald 1 up

Jason Dufner & Zach Johnson lost to Rory McIlroy & Ian Poulter 1 up

Match score: USA 10–6 Europe

Sunday singles: USA 3½–8½ Europe

Bubba Watson lost to Luke Donald 2&1

Webb Simpson lost to Ian Poulter 2 up

Keegan Bradley lost to Rory McIlroy 2&1

Phil Mickelson lost to Justin Rose 1 up

Brandt Snedeker lost to Paul Lawrie 5&3

Dustin Johnson beat Nicolas Colsaerts 3&2

Zach Johnson beat Graeme McDowell 2&1

Jim Furyk lost to Sergio García 1 up

Jason Dufner beat Peter Hanson 2 up

Matt Kuchar lost to Lee Westwood 3&2

Steve Stricker lost to Martin Kaymer 1 up

Tiger Woods halved with Francesco Molinari

Final match score: USA 13½–14½ Europe

Europe retains the Ryder Cup

Credits

Extracts from the following have been replicated in this book: